JESUS CHRIST FOR TODAY

D0166615

LIBRARY OF LIVING FAITH

JOHN M. MULDER, General Editor

JESUS CHRIST
FOR
TODAY

BY
GEORGE W. STROUP

THE WESTMINSTER PRESS
PHILADELPHIA

Scripture quotations from the Revised Standard Version of
the Bible are copyrighted 1946, 1952, © 1971, 1973 by the
Division of Christian Education of the National Council of
Churches of Christ in the U.S.A., and are used by permis-
sion.

BOOK DESIGN BY DOROTHY ALDEN SMITH

First edition

Published by The Westminster Press®
Philadelphia, Pennsylvania

PRINTED IN THE UNITED STATES OF AMERICA
9 8 7 6 5 4 3 2 1

Quotation from "Choruses from 'The Rock'" is reprinted by per-
mission of Harcourt Brace Jovanovich, Inc., from *Collected Poems
1909–1962*, by T. S. Eliot, copyright 1936 by Harcourt Brace
Jovanovich, Inc.; copyright © 1963, 1964 by T. S. Eliot.

Library of Congress Cataloging in Publication Data

Stroup, George W., 1944–
Jesus Christ for today.

(Library of living faith)
Bibliography: p.
1. Jesus Christ—Person and offices. I. Title.
II. Series.
BT202.S83 1982   232   82-13494
ISBN 0-664-24450-5 (pbk.)

CONTENTS

FOREWORD

The word "theology" comes from two Greek words—*theos* ("God") and *logos* ("word" or "thought"). Theology is simply words about God or thinking about God. But for many Christians, theology is remote, abstract, baffling, confusing, and boring. They turn it over to the professionals—the theologians—who can ponder and inquire into the ways of God with the world.

This series, Library of Living Faith, is for those Christians who thought theology wasn't for them. It is a collection of ten books on crucial doctrines or issues in the Christian faith today. Each book attempts to show why our theology—our thoughts about God—matters in what we do and say as Christians. The series is an invitation to readers to become theologians themselves—to reflect on the Bible and on the history of the church and to find their own ways of understanding the grace of God in Jesus Christ.

The Library of Living Faith is in the tradition of another series published by Westminster Press in the 1950s, the Layman's Theological Library. This new collection of volumes tries to serve the church in the challenges of the closing decades of this century.

The ten books are based on the affirmation of the Letter to the Ephesians (4:4–6): "There is one body and one

Spirit, just as you were called to the one hope that belongs
to your call, one Lord, one faith, one baptism, one God and
Father of us all, who is above all and through all and in all."
Each book addresses a particular theme as part of the
Christian faith as a whole; each book speaks to the church
as a whole. Theology is too important to be left only to the
theologians; it is the work and witness of the entire people
of God.

But, as Ephesians says, "grace was given to each of us
according to the measure of Christ's gift" (Eph. 4:7), and
the Library of Living Faith tries to demonstrate the diversity of theology in the church today. Differences, of course,
are not unique to American Christianity. One only needs
to look at the New Testament and the early church to see
how "the measure of Christ's gift" produced disagreement
and conflict as well as a rich variety of understandings of
Christian faith and discipleship. In the midst of the unity
of the faith, there has never been uniformity. The authors
in this series have their own points of view, and readers
may argue along the way with the authors' interpretations. But each book presents varying points of view and
shows what difference it makes to take a particular theological position. Sparks may fly, but the result, we hope,
will be a renewed vision of what it means to be a Christian
exhibiting in the world today a living faith.

These books are also intended to be a library—a set of
books that should be read together. Of course, not everything is included. As the Gospel of John puts it, "There are
also many other things which Jesus did; were every one of
them to be written, I suppose that the world itself could
not contain the books that would be written" (John 21:25).
Readers should not be content to read just the volume on
Jesus Christ or on God or on the Holy Spirit and leave out
those on the church or on the Christian life or on Christianity's relationship with other faiths. For we are called to
one faith with many parts.

The volumes are also designed to be read by groups of people. Writing may be a lonely task, but the literature of the church was never intended for individuals alone. It is for the entire body of Christ. Through discussion and even debate, the outlines of a living faith can emerge.

This book takes its title and theme from Dietrich Bonhoeffer's famous query: "What is bothering me incessantly is the question what Christianity really is, or indeed who Christ really is, for us today" *(Letters and Papers from Prison).* Bonhoeffer asked that question in jail under the Nazi regime, but the question is not new. Even Jesus asked his disciples, "But who do you say that I am?" (Matt. 16:15). Each age has found it necessary to come to terms anew with the identity of Jesus Christ, for in answering that question, Christians define the heart of their faith. George Stroup outlines the various ways in which Christians have answered this question throughout the history of the church and offers his own understanding of how the church can view Jesus Christ today. Dr. Stroup teaches theology at Austin Presbyterian Theological Seminary. He holds degrees from Rice, Yale, and Vanderbilt Universities, and he is the author of *The Promise of Narrative Theology: Recovering the Gospel in the Church,* as well as several articles and essays. When he isn't thinking about theology, he plays a mean game of racketball.

JOHN M. MULDER

Louisville Presbyterian Theological Seminary
Louisville, Kentucky

1
JESUS CHRIST
AND CHRISTIAN FAITH

Who is Jesus of Nazareth? Why do Christians call Jesus the Christ? And why do they call Jesus their Savior? These three questions have often been asked by both Christians and non-Christians. They are perennial questions, by no means peculiar to people living at a particular place and time in history. They go to the very heart of Christian faith, and they will probably continue to be asked as long as people inquire into the meaning of Christian faith and life. This book explores these three questions and some of the ways in which the Christian community has answered them.

From its beginning in the first century, the church has heard these three questions about Jesus of Nazareth posed in various forms, and has attempted to respond with coherent and consistent theological affirmations—what the church calls creeds and confessions. On the basis of the witness of Scripture and its claims about Jesus, the church has formulated theological statements by which it articulates and clarifies the faith it confesses.

The church has tried to write creeds and confessions that are consistent both with Scripture, the church's primary resource, and with what the church has confessed through the ages. At the same time, by means of these creeds and confessions the church has tried to answer new questions and to speak intelligibly to new cultural situations. It is this latter consideration—the concern that the church's confession of faith be responsive and intelligible —which makes theological reflection about Jesus Christ both terribly difficult and extremely important. Although the church has recognized the importance of being faithful to the witness of Scripture and being guided and instructed by the church's faith and experience through history, it also has recognized that questions about the identity and meaning of Jesus Christ are always asked from a particular context, and that the church's answers must speak intelligibly to that situation. Consequently, most churches have been unwilling simply to repeat the same creeds and confessions in response to every question asked about Jesus Christ. The church has confessed its faith by means of different forms of language, and it has employed various terms and idioms to make its faith intelligible to the culture in which it finds itself.

If one reads through the confessions of most Christian denominations, it is obvious that the church has used very different forms of language to confess its faith in the God who raised Jesus from the dead. It has used language it hoped would address serious, honest questions about Jesus Christ. For example, the Nicene Creed, one of the church's earliest creeds, describes Jesus Christ as

> the only-begotten Son of God, begotten of the Father before all worlds, God of God, Light of Light, Very God of Very God, begotten, not made, being of one substance with the Father by whom all things were made . . .

But the United Presbyterian Church's Confession of 1967 avoids the language of "substance" and emphasizes the humanity and ministry of Jesus Christ. It declares that Jesus was

> a Palestinian Jew, lived among his own people and shared their needs, temptations, joys, and sorrows. He expressed

the love of God in word and deed and became a brother to all kinds of sinful men. But his complete obedience led him into conflict with his people. His life and teaching judged their goodness, religious aspirations, and national hopes. Many rejected him and demanded his death. In giving himself freely for them he took upon himself the judgment under which all men stand convicted. God raised him from the dead, vindicating him as Messiah and Lord.

One of these theological statements about Jesus Christ is not necessarily "better" or more truthful than the other. The meaning of each has to be assessed in the light of the religious and cultural situation which the two statements address. They each attempt to make Christian claims about Jesus Christ meaningful to a particular cultural situation—the Nicene Creed in the fourth century and the Confession of 1967 in the twentieth—in the light of the witness of Scripture and the faith of the church.

Furthermore, the church has always believed that the central reality—the grace of God's Word in Jesus Christ—is not a historical artifact. Rather, that Word is a living reality that continues to speak to the life of the church and the world. Part of the church's task is its commission to listen for God's Word in Jesus Christ and to speak that Word to the world. The church cannot do that simply by repeating old confessions. The church is faithful to its commission only when it continues to listen for God's graceful yet disturbing Word in Jesus Christ.

Perhaps it was this conviction that led the German theologian and martyr Dietrich Bonhoeffer to write from his prison cell, "What is bothering me incessantly is the question what Christianity really is, or indeed who Christ really is, for us today." Bonhoeffer did not ask that question out of ignorance of what the church had said about Jesus Christ in the past or out of despair that Jesus Christ no longer was significant for life in the twentieth century. Bonhoeffer asked that question because he believed that God continues to address the world through Jesus Christ and that Christian faith and life must attend to this Jesus if it is to be faithful to the God it worships.

THE CENTER OF CHRISTIAN FAITH

Bonhoeffer's question—what is Christianity and who is Jesus Christ for us today?—deserves serious reflection. In the first place, Bonhoeffer points to what the church has recognized throughout its history—that the "essence" or central reality of Christian faith is directly related to the person of Jesus of Nazareth. Jesus himself gives Christian faith its distinctive shape. In order to answer the question, "What is Christianity?" the church has pointed to Jesus of Nazareth and what God has done "in" him. Secondly, Bonhoeffer reminds us that, although Christians throughout history are united in their common confession that Jesus is Lord, the Lordship of Jesus may mean different forms of discipleship in different periods of history.

Christians believe that Jesus Christ is always "for us," but the sense in which he is for us and what his call to discipleship means cannot be determined apart from the context of different situations. Christians believe that the meaning of life is found in a relationship to that ultimate reality they call "God," a reality they believe they have encountered in the person of a first-century Jew named Jesus. In him they believe they know God to be gracious, loving, and faithful. Jesus of Nazareth, therefore, is the center of Christian faith. He is the basis, the foundation, for what Christians claim they know about God; he is the reason Christians attempt to live lives that reflect something of the grace and love of God; and he is the basis for their hope in God's faithfulness and their trust that the future belongs to God and is to be awaited in confidence rather than in despair.

Christian faith can be compared to a prism. Just as a single prism has many faces, so too there are many different but related realities that make up Christian faith. At an intellectual level, these different realities of Christian faith are called "doctrine." Christians believe that Jesus Christ is the light that passes through the prism of Christian faith and enables them to see the meaning of realities such as God, sin, forgiveness, love, and kingdom. Although Christian faith is finally an act of trust in God's grace, Christians believe that it is Jesus of Nazareth who discloses the true reality of God, the meaning of God's love, and the nature of God's kingdom. He allows Christians to see what these things are in themselves and in their relation to one another.

But while Jesus of Nazareth may be the central reality for how Christians understand God and life lived in response to God's grace, Jesus has been and continues to be an elusive figure for both Christians and non-Christians. Jesus has been understood in very different ways by Christian communities in the past, and even in contemporary Christian communities Jesus appears to have a remarkable variety of faces. For example, Christians who belong to conservative political and religious movements in the United States often talk about Jesus in primarily moral categories that stress the value of human life, the sanctity of the individual, the evils of moral behavior that deviates from traditional norms, and the defense of middle-class, white society. On the other hand, some small Christian communities in Latin America and other parts of the third world described a very different Jesus. Their Jesus takes the side of the poor and the oppressed in their struggle against social and corporate forms of evil. And their Jesus calls all Christians to participate in this struggle in order that witness may be given to the meaning of the cross and the coming of God's kingdom. Christians of a conservative political and religious persuasion point to texts in the New Testament such as Jesus' claim, "My kingship is not of this world," and his admonition, "Do not labor for the food which perishes, but for the food which endures to eternal life" (John 6:27). On the other hand, Christians who are sympathetic to liberation movements point to different biblical texts, such as the one in which Jesus describes a day of judgment when the Son of Man will separate humanity on the basis of its response to him:

> Then he will say to those at his left hand, "Depart from me, you cursed, into the eternal fire prepared for the devil and his angels; for I was hungry and you gave me no food, I was thirsty and you gave me no drink, I was a stranger and you did not welcome me, naked and you did not clothe me, sick and in prison and you did not visit me." Then they also will answer, "Lord, when did we see thee hungry or thirsty or a stranger or naked or sick or in prison, and did not minister to thee?" Then he will answer them, "Truly, I say to you, as you did it not to one of the least of these, you did it not to me." (Matt. 25:41–45)

To those who stand outside the Christian community and merely observe the speech and behavior of Christians, it is not clear how these two very different interpretations of Jesus of Nazareth refer to the same individual. Not only are these two pictures of Jesus quite different, but the interpretations of Christian faith and life accompanying them also differ significantly. In some cases the differences in these interpretations of the identity of Jesus of Nazareth and the meaning of Christian faith are so great that it is not clear how these two communities can both be described as "Christian." In the minds of some interpreters of Christianity these diverse pictures of Jesus raise the question of whether Jesus Christ actually is the center of Christian faith.

For four reasons, however, most Christians continue to insist that despite the various ways in which Jesus is understood, he remains the central reality of Christian faith. These four reasons are that Jesus of Nazareth allows people to see the true nature of God, Jesus Christ defines the meaning of salvation, Jesus provides Christian individuals their final and true identity, and Jesus defines the nature and mission of the church. These four reasons require some reflection.

JESUS AND GOD

Christian faith is earthy, this-worldly, specific, and particular. It is not primarily a set of philosophical principles, a world view, a metaphysics, or a moral system. It is rooted in the conviction that the reality that Christians call God became visible and was encountered in those historical events which make up the personal identity of Jesus of Nazareth. Christians do not believe their faith is abstract; they understand it to be read off the face and life of a specific person who lived at a particular point in time and space. The First Letter of John makes the same point:

> That which was from the beginning, which we have heard, which we have seen with our eyes, which we have looked upon and touched with our hands, concerning the word of life—the life was made manifest, and we saw it, and testify to it, and proclaim to you the eternal life which was with the Father and was made manifest to us. (I John 1:1–2)

There is nothing abstract here about the love of God. The claim that Christians should "love one another; for love is of God, and he who loves is born of God and knows God" (I John 4:7) follows from the conviction that the reality of God has been heard, seen, looked upon, and touched in the person of Jesus of Nazareth. Jesus is the indispensable center of Christian faith because he is the specific, visible representation of God.

The technical term that Christians use to make this confession is "incarnation." This Jesus makes God a tangible, earthy reality. To look for the center of Christian faith somewhere else than in Jesus is to make that faith less specific and more abstract than Christians believe it is. The basis for Christian faith is not an idea or a set of principles but a person—Jesus Christ. In him, Christians believe they encounter the grace and love of God.

Although the incarnation is vitally important for understanding why Jesus of Nazareth is the center of Christian faith, it is possible to misinterpret the incarnation in such a way that it distorts faith's most basic claims. While Jesus of Nazareth is the center of faith, he is not a second god or a substitute for God. In some Christian communities, especially in the United States, not only is Jesus the foundation for statements about God but Jesus becomes the sole object of worship. It is one thing to say that the Word of God is heard and seen in Jesus of Nazareth, or to say with the apostle Paul that "in Christ God was reconciling the world to himself" (II Cor. 5:19). It is something else to describe Jesus as the sole agent of reconciliation. When Jesus prays in Gethsemane, "Abba, Father, all things are possible to thee; remove this cup from me; yet not what I will, but what thou wilt" (Mark 14:36), he is not talking to himself. Similarly, Christians traditionally have claimed that the good news of Easter is that God raised Jesus from the dead, which is not the same thing as the claim that Jesus raised himself from the dead.

While the Christian doctrine of the incarnation points to the unique and crucial importance of Jesus of Nazareth for understanding God, Christianity is not and must not be allowed to become what some theologians have colorfully described as "Jesusolatry." Jesus of Nazareth is the incarnation of God's Word, the reality of God made visible, audible, and tangible in history, but Jesus does not replace God. The significance of the Christian doctrine of the Trinity (that the one God consists of the three Persons: Father, Son, and Spirit) is that it points to Jesus as the incarnation of the reality of God and the foundation of human knowledge about God; but the doctrine of the Trinity also declares that it is the love and grace *of God* which Christians believe they see and encounter in this

Jesus. Historically, of course, questions about the relation between Jesus and God were what prompted the early church to formulate its doctrine of the Trinity. Although this doctrine affirms that in Jesus of Nazareth the world encounters the very reality of God, it also affirms that the object of Christian worship (the personal reality in whom Christian faith trusts) is the God revealed in the life and ministry of Jesus. It is not accidental that many of the churches which come close to Jesusolatry also have purged any mention of the Trinity from their hymns and liturgy. Such a misrepresentation of Jesus' relation to God is contrary to Scripture and to the major confessional documents of the church.

Christians believe that Jesus of Nazareth is the visible re-presentation of the reality of God, or, to use a phrase that such contemporary theologians as John A. T. Robinson and Hans Küng have employed, Jesus is "the human face of God." It is the very human face of Jesus which is the basis of the specific, tangible, earthy understanding Christians have of the grace and love of God.

JESUS AND THE MEANING OF SALVATION

Jesus is the indispensable center of Christian faith, not only because he is the basis for what Christians claim they know about God but also because he is the basis of their understanding of salvation. Many Christians would agree that II Cor. 5:19 ("in Christ God was reconciling the world to himself") is a summary of the gospel. That text demonstrates that there are two foci to Christian faith, both of which are necessary for an adequate interpretation of the gospel. On the one hand, as we have seen, faith confesses that the Word of God has become visible in Jesus of Nazareth. The incarnation is not, however, an end in itself. The Word of God became visible in Jesus of Nazareth in order that the world might be reconciled to God. If the incarnation is not understood in relation to what Christians mean by salvation and reconciliation, it becomes an interesting but finally irrelevant religious mystery. God's reconciliation of the world makes the incarnation relevant and meaningful.

Here we encounter one of the most important claims of Christian faith. We cannot understand who Jesus was and is unless we understand his significance for us. At issue, of course, is the Christian conviction that the fundamental human problem is sin. By "sin" Christians mean the destruction of the one relation which is most important to every person—one's relation to God. To be "in sin" (and all people are) is both to live in a world that is estranged from God and to engage in acts that further estrange us from God and other people.

In the life and death of Jesus Christ, Christians believe that God overcomes the brokenness of human sin and that they are reconciled to God and to one another. The technical term that Christians use to describe this reality is "atonement." Because of who Jesus is and what Jesus does, Christians are redeemed from the despair of a broken world and given a new life of faith, hope, and love. It was this conviction that led Philip Melanchthon in the sixteenth century to argue that "to know Christ means to know his benefits." He asked: "Unless you know why Christ put on flesh and was nailed to the cross, what good will it do you to know merely the history about him?"

The Christian confession that "God was in Christ" gives salvation its distinctive shape, and, most important, it declares that salvation has not taken place in some distant location but has become a reality in the midst of human history. It is visible and accessible to all people. The incarnation enables us to claim that God's gracious act of reconciliation has taken place in human history and consequently is a reality for all people.

Not only is Jesus the basis for what Christians know

about God; he also points to the distinctive feature of this knowledge—that it is "unto salvation." Hence, the knowledge of God that Christians have in Jesus Christ is a peculiar sort. It is not just "objective" knowledge, such as my knowledge of the number of moons that revolve around Saturn. It is also knowledge that alters my understanding of who I am and what kind of person I am. It is knowledge that leads me to a decision. Either what Christians claim about God on the basis of Jesus of Nazareth is not true, and the gospel is not good news, or it is true and should lead to conversion and transformation. If what Christians claim to know about God is true, then it is not just one more piece of information that a person can add to his or her collection of important data. To know the grace and love of God present in Jesus of Nazareth is also to experience the transforming power of that grace and love, to discover oneself to be what the apostle Paul called a "new creation."

When Christians look at the life story of Jesus of Nazareth, they believe they see the drama of God's redemption of the world. Such knowledge is neither abstract nor speculative. It is intensely personal and world-transforming knowledge. Jesus is indispensable for understanding faith because what we know in and by means of him is the grace and love of God, a grace that redeems us from personal and social forms of brokenness and calls us to a life of discipleship, which the New Testament refers to as a "ministry of reconciliation."

What we know in faith leads us to a life of love and freedom. And just as Jesus of Nazareth is the basis for what Christians know about God, so too he defines the meaning of Christian love and freedom. Unfortunately, these phrases—"Christian love" and "Christian freedom"—have become so familiar to contemporary culture that they have lost their sting and their proper offensiveness. They have been domesticated and made acceptable by

"Christian" societies whose structures and policies explicitly deny the reality of Christian love and freedom. In modern culture, fiction often speaks the truth of Christian faith clearly and unequivocally. In Flannery O'Connor's short story "A Good Man Is Hard to Find," an escaped convict, appropriately named The Misfit, states the truth of the matter moments before he murders an elderly grandmother:

> "Jesus was the only One that ever raised the dead," The Misfit continued, "and He shouldn't have done it. He thrown everything off balance. If He did what He said, then it's nothing for you to do but throw away everything and follow Him, and if He didn't, then it's nothing for you to do but enjoy the few minutes you got left the best way you can —by killing somebody or burning down his house or doing some other meanness to him. No pleasure but meanness," he said and his voice had become almost a snarl.

The Misfit sees quite clearly that what Christians claim they know about God is neither speculative nor disinterested knowledge. If what they claim they know is true, then the only proper response is an act of radical trust (which Christians refer to as "faith") and a life of love and freedom in witness to Jesus' cross, a life in which everything is indeed "thrown off balance," if life is measured by what Paul calls "the wisdom of the world."

Christians believe that in Jesus of Nazareth they can not only know the meaning of salvation but also experience its reality in the love, freedom, and reconciliation set loose in the world by Jesus' cross and resurrection. Salvation is just as earthy, this-worldly, and specific as is the first-century Jew, Jesus of Nazareth.

JESUS AND CHRISTIAN IDENTITY

Not only does Jesus allow the world to see the reality of God and understand and experience the meaning of salvation; he also defines the shape of the life and identity to which Christians are called. In the process of trusting in God and living lives that reflect something of the radical nature of faith, Christians claim that they also experience something else, something they refer to as "being conformed to Christ" or "living in Christ." We have noted that what Christians claim they know in and by means of Jesus is never simply facts or data that have nothing to do with the identity of the knower. On the contrary, what they know demands an act of faith; it holds out the hope of new life; most important, it calls them to a particular form of life in the world. Christians sometimes refer to this distinctive form of life as "discipleship." To know Jesus as the human face of God and to see the love and grace of God in him is at the same time to be called to a different way of being in the world. Christian discipleship, life lived in response to Jesus of Nazareth, has a definite form or shape about it, which it receives from the one it calls "Lord." Because Jesus of Nazareth defines the shape and meaning of discipleship, Christians find it impossible to describe their faith or what they understand themselves to be doing in the world without referring to Jesus.

Three implications of the relation between Jesus and the life of discipleship are especially important for understanding the nature of Christian identity. In the first place, the love and freedom which we see in Jesus frees us from a self-centered existence, which shows itself in various forms of pride and selfishness, and reminds us that true life is lived in radical dependence on the grace of God. One of the most powerful statements of this conviction is John Calvin's comment on I Cor. 6:19–20, where Paul says, "You are not your own; you were bought with a price." Calvin wrote:

> We are not our own: let not our reason nor our will, therefore, sway our plans and deeds. We are not our own: let us

therefore not set it as our goal to seek what is expedient for us according to the flesh. . . . Conversely, we are God's: let us therefore live for him and die for him. We are God's: let his wisdom and will therefore rule all our actions. We are God's: let all the parts of our life accordingly strive toward him as our only lawful goal [Rom. 14:8; cf. I Cor. 6:19].

Second, to be a disciple of Jesus is to experience one's life as having been turned around and transformed. Christians call this experience "conversion," and it can assume a variety of forms. It can refer to specific, dramatic moments, such as that moment in the parable of the prodigal son (Luke 15:11–32) when the son "came to himself" and returned from the far country to his father's home. Or it can refer to the transformation that takes place over the course of a lifetime, in which God's grace overcomes an individual's self-centeredness and frees that person to live in obedience to Jesus of Nazareth. In either case, Christian discipleship means that a person's identity has been transformed by Jesus of Nazareth and is in the process of being conformed to him.

Christian faith is not simply something that one adds to life as though it were yet another piece of baggage one has decided to carry. The New Testament makes it very clear that the act of faith, the decision to trust the God revealed in Jesus of Nazareth, is a radical act which leads the Christian in new directions. The Gospel of Mark, for example, tells the story of a rich man who asked Jesus what he had to do to inherit eternal life (Mark 10:17–22). He told Jesus that he had observed the commandments of the law since his youth. But when Jesus told him to do one final thing—"go, sell what you have, and give to the poor, and you will have treasure in heaven; and come, follow me"—the rich man went away in sorrow, "for he had great possessions." The point of Mark's story is not that all Christians must sell their possessions, but that Christian discipleship is not simply an additional responsibility, like membership in a local civic club. It is a commitment that leads one in new directions and can be pursued only by means of God's grace and determined single-mindedness.

Third, Christian identity is profoundly relational. The nature of Christian identity is that we know we stand finally and ultimately in relation to God, and it is the relation between us and God that gives us our true and lasting identity. For the apostle Paul, true self-knowledge comes at the end of time, when we stand face-to-face with God:

> For now we see in a mirror dimly, but then face to face. Now I know in part; then I shall understand fully, even as I have been fully understood. (I Cor. 13:12)

At the end of the fourth century, Augustine used this text from Paul to begin his reflections on the nature of memory in his *Confessions:* "Let me know you, for you are the God who knows me; *let me recognize you as you have recognized me.*" For Christian faith the face of God is seen in the face of Jesus of Nazareth. But here there is an important tension in Christian identity. On the one hand, Christians claim that our true identity is to be found in our relation to God. On the other hand, they also say that we do not really know God unless we know how God is related to us. In other words, Christian identity has two equally important sides to it. We know ourselves only when we understand our relation to God. And we understand what Christians mean by God only when God becomes the one who is our creator and redeemer. These two sides to Christian identity are intelligible only in the one person, Jesus of Nazareth. In him, Christians know both the true nature of humanity and the true nature of God.

Perhaps the closest human analogy to this Christian claim is what some people experience in a marriage or an especially close friendship. I may discover dimensions of myself that were hitherto hidden from me, in my relationship to my spouse or friend. In the extended experience of loving and being loved, I discover truths about myself, both good and bad, which come to light only in the depth of human relationships. Some of the most important things about myself I discover only in my relationship to others. And Christians, of course, confess that the deepest truths about ourselves are unveiled in our encounter with and relationship to Jesus Christ.

Apart from Jesus, therefore, Christian faith has no center, shape, or focus. Jesus is the light in the prism of faith who enables us to see the nature of God, understand the meaning of salvation, and, finally, know the true meaning of our own identity. Jesus Christ is nothing less than the spectacles through which we see and understand reality.

JESUS AND THE CHURCH

Not only does Jesus of Nazareth serve as the basis for the reconstruction of personal identity but he also gives the Christian church its corporate identity. The two are, of course, interrelated. To be a Christian is indeed to have one's personal identity altered and transformed by the grace of God in Jesus of Nazareth. At the same time, to be baptized into the life and death of Jesus Christ is to become a part of his "body," the visible representation of which is the church.

Christian identity is life lived in the context of the church, the body of Christ and the people of God. But Christians have long realized that they must be careful about the relation between Jesus and the church. Although Christian identity has two sides, the relation between Jesus and the church has only one side. The church does not exist as an end in itself. It exists for one reason— to witness to God's reconciling work in Jesus. Whenever the mere existence of the church becomes more important than the task it is called to perform, then the meaning and practice of Christian faith have become distorted.

The church does not define who Jesus is; rather, Jesus defines who the church is and what it is called to be and do. This conviction was an important part of the 1934 declaration of the Confessional Synod of the German Evangelical Church, "The Theological Declaration of Barmen." Confronted with the stark reality of Hitler's Third Reich and that government's demand that German Christians pledge their loyalty to their country, some Christians in Germany felt compelled to state unequivocally that Jesus Christ alone is Lord of the church:

> The Christian Church is the congregation of the brethren in which Jesus Christ acts presently as the Lord in Word and sacrament through the Holy Spirit. As the Church of pardoned sinners, it has to testify in the midst of a sinful world, with its message as with its order, that it is solely his property, and that it lives and wants to live solely from his comfort and from his direction in the expectation of his appearance.

Jesus gives direction and therein identity to the Christian community. In the words of the Gospel of John, Jesus is "the way, and the truth, and the life" (John 14:6), and as such he shows the church where it is to be and what it is to do in the world.

In recent years, the church has been a major topic of discussion in Christian circles. But in practically every case, Christians came to the conclusion that it was not possible to discuss what the church is or what it should be doing in the world without first discussing the church's relation to Jesus of Nazareth. In the language of Christian doctrine, it soon became apparent that questions of "ecclesiology" (the doctrine of the church) could not be resolved unless attention first was given to "Christology" (the doctrine of the person and work of Jesus Christ). Jesus is the basis for both the identity of Christian individuals and the identity of Christian communities.

It is important to insist that it is Jesus who gives the

church its true identity, because the church is always tempted to forget who has called it into existence and whom it serves. The claim that Jesus is Lord of all things, including the church, gives the church a principle by which it can measure its faithfulness. The issue of faithfulness is just as important to the church as it is to Israel. One of the great fears of the writers of the Old Testament, especially the authors of Deuteronomy, was that Israel would forget the God who brought it out of bondage in Egypt and led it into a land flowing with milk and honey, and that when life became comfortable, Israel would turn to other gods and no longer worship Yahweh. In order to avoid this fate, the writers of Deuteronomy repeatedly urge Israel to remember its history with God. Similarly, the apostle Paul urges the Christians at Corinth to celebrate the Lord's Supper by remembering the story which is the setting for the Supper:

> For I received from the Lord what I also delivered to you, that the Lord Jesus on the night when he was betrayed took bread, and when he had given thanks, he broke it, and said, "This is my body which is for you. Do this in remembrance of me." (I Cor. 11:23–24)

Only insofar as the church finds its identity in Jesus of Nazareth will it be faithful to the gospel it confesses and proclaims. Jesus of Nazareth gives the church its true identity, sustains and encourages it, and also stands over against it, calling it to faithful discipleship in the world. The church belongs to Jesus and not he to it. That is why Christians sing:

> The church's one foundation is Jesus Christ
> her Lord;
> She is his new creation by water and the word:
> From heaven he came and sought her to be his holy
> bride;
> With his own blood he bought her, and for her
> life he died.

Christian thinking about faith and life finds itself constantly returning to Jesus of Nazareth in order to find its way in the world. Christian faith loses its way and becomes confused only when it no longer looks to its center and the cross that stands there. Jesus Christ is the means by which Christians understand what faith has been, and he is the means by which Christians will understand what faith will be in the future. Christian thinking begins and ends with Jesus of Nazareth.

2
THE JESUS OF THE SCRIPTURES

Christian reflection about Jesus of Nazareth must begin with the Bible. Our knowledge of the historical person, Jesus of Nazareth, is for all practical purposes limited to what Scripture tells us about him. Although there are brief allusions to Jesus in other literature from the first century, the New Testament gives us the only substantial picture we have of the so-called "historical Jesus."

When Christians think about Jesus they must begin with Scripture's description of him. The claim that salvation is defined by Jesus drives Christians to Scripture, because it is only there that they have access to the Jesus of history.

In the history of the Christian church, there have been many attempts to discover the conclusive portrait of the Jesus of history. None of these "conclusive" historical portraits, however, has gained popular approval. Historical and theological scholarship has eventually shown each of them to be unreliable. But despite repeated setbacks, the search for the historical Jesus continues to this day and probably always will continue. With the emergence of new forms of science and knowledge and the collapse of familiar, established structures and institutions, the question of the distinctiveness of Christianity has often assumed a special urgency and prompted Christians to search for the permanent, enduring shape of Christian faith in the historical figure who is the center of faith. In practically every case, the search for the historical Jesus has been motivated by faith in search of genuine understanding, not idle curiosity or perverse destructiveness.

BIBLICAL FAITH AND HISTORICAL FACT

Despite the best intentions of those who have engaged in the search for the historical Jesus, the results have usually been disappointing. The problem is that those who search Scripture for the historical Jesus often ask questions that Scripture has no interest in answering. That is not to say that Scripture is uninterested in questions of fact and history. On the contrary, most of the writers of the New Testament insist that the gospel they have received and are passing on refers to particular historical events. The apostle Paul states this explicitly in his correspondence with the church at Corinth:

> For I delivered to you as of first importance what I also received, that Christ died for our sins in accordance with the scriptures, that he was buried, that he was raised on the third day in accordance with the scriptures, and that he appeared to Cephas, then to the twelve. (I Cor. 15:3–5)

But while Christians understand faith to refer to historical events, such as the crucifixion and resurrection of Jesus, the writers of Scripture have a curious relation to those historical events. They understand faith to be based on historical events, but they seem far more interested in what the facts *mean* than in the facts themselves. In one sense of the word, the writers of the New Testament are not historians. They do not have the professional historian's concern for historical accuracy (a kind of Joe Friday preoccupation with "just the facts, Ma'am"). In fact, the New Testament writers seem unconcerned whether their version of a story differs from that of other New Testament writers. For example, if we examine the description of the empty tomb in Matthew 28, Mark 16, Luke 24, and John 20, it is clear that the Gospel writers differ about the facts. They do not agree on which women went to the tomb, what they found there, how many angels were at the tomb, and what the women did after they found the tomb empty.

On the other hand, the writers of the New Testament are not primarily historians. Their faith rests on the interpretation of certain historical events ("in accordance with the scriptures"). The New Testament authors are historians only secondarily. First and foremost, they are pastors and preachers with a gospel, or "good news," to share with other Christians and the rest of the world. The good news to them is not how many women found the tomb empty, but the amazing claim that God raised Jesus of Nazareth from the dead. The good news is not whether there were one or two angels in the tomb, but the startling assertion that the crucified Jesus is the risen Christ.

This distinction between Gospel faith and historical fact can create frustration for modern readers of the New Testament. Many modern readers go to the New Testament wanting to know only what happened. When they pose that question to the biblical text, they are often disappointed. The New Testament wants the reader to learn the good news about God's vindication of Jesus, and it wants the reader to make the appropriate response of faith and discipleship. For the modern reader to pose historical questions to the New Testament is to ask questions that it was not designed to answer.

The Gospels in the New Testament are not, strictly speaking, biographies or "lives of Jesus." They omit much, if not most, of Jesus' history, and they tell us virtually nothing about Jesus' intentions, interests, and motivation. We learn little from the Gospels about Jesus' childhood or life prior to his baptism by John. And even in that brief period of time when he carried on his ministry in Galilee and Jerusalem, the New Testament says very little about Jesus' intentions and motives. The Gospels are not biographies of Jesus, but proclamation of the good news that Jesus is the Christ and that in him God has reconciled the world to himself. We cannot read the Gospels the same way as we read a biography of Abraham Lincoln or a historical account of the Civil War. Indeed, if we read the Gospels to find the proper chronology of events or to determine the historical details surrounding each part of the story, we may well miss the one thing the Gospels are trying to tell us.

Furthermore, neither the Gospels nor the rest of the New Testament was written for the world or for posterity. In most cases, the Gospels and the letters of the New Testament were written to interpret the meaning of Christian faith for communities facing specific problems at a given point in history. Although there is some scholarly disagreement about the precise nature of the situations and the communities addressed by the Gospels, it is clear that specific concerns deeply influence the structure and content of each of them. Jesus assumes a different appearance in each of the Gospels, and the interpretation of his teaching and ministry varies from one Gospel to the next.

In Mark's Gospel, for example, Jesus appears abruptly at the beginning of the Gospel, is baptized by John the Baptist, and announces that "The time is fulfilled, and the kingdom of God is at hand; repent, and believe in the gospel" (Mark 1:15). Mark's Jesus carries out his ministry with a sense of urgency; very soon the Son of man will come "in clouds with great power and glory" (Mark 13:26) to gather his elect. Also, Mark leaves the reader in some doubt, at least until the final event of the cross, as to Jesus' true identity and what it means to call him the Son of God.

In John's Gospel, on the other hand, Jesus is portrayed quite differently than in Mark. John's Jesus has little to say about a coming kingdom of God. His message draws attention to himself: "I and the Father are one" (John 10:30); "he who sees me sees him who sent me" (12:45); and "I am the bread of life; he who comes to me shall not hunger, and he who believes in me shall never thirst" (6:35). The differences between Mark's Jesus and John's Jesus pose several questions for Christian faith. The problem is not just that many of the words that John's Jesus speaks appear nowhere in Mark, nor in Matthew and Luke, but that—even more important—John's Jesus seems to have a different understanding of himself and his mission than does Mark's Jesus. If Mark and John were writing biographies of Jesus, we would have serious questions about the apparent differences in their descriptions of Jesus. But that is not what either of them intends. They are both interpreting the meaning of the basic Christian confession that "Jesus is Lord" for specific Christian communities facing difficult questions concerning the meaning of faithful discipleship. The differences in their descriptions of Jesus have to be understood, at least in part, in terms of the questions and situations they are addressing.

Although we cannot overlook the differences in the descriptions of Jesus in the Gospels, there are also some striking similarities between them. One of the most important of these is that all the Gospels are written from the perspective of the Easter faith of the Christian community; that is, the Gospels are written from our side of that event which we refer to as the resurrection of Jesus Christ. That is perhaps the major reason that the writers of the Gospels do not tell their story dispassionately and disinterestedly. Each of them shares the conviction that God has raised Jesus of Nazareth from the dead and that this Jesus is the long-awaited Christ.

The writers of the New Testament are totally involved in what they have to say. Their interpretation of who Jesus is and what he calls the church to be and to do is decisively shaped by their Easter faith and experience. A proper interpretation of the Gospels requires that the reader take account of the writers' Easter faith. Modern biblical scholarship has demonstrated that some of the sayings put in Jesus' mouth by the writers of the Gospels may not have been uttered by Jesus, but are a reflection of the writers' Easter faith and their confession that Jesus is the Christ. Many of the sayings in John's Gospel, for example, are suspected of being reflections of Johannine faith rather than actual words of Jesus.

The discovery of the role of Easter faith in the composition of the Gospels is one more reason why many interpreters of the New Testament insist that it cannot be read as biography or as "objective" history. What one reads in the Gospels is the proclamation of the Easter faith of the text's writers and not a historical reconstruction of Jesus of Nazareth. This discovery of the confessional and kerygmatic nature of the Gospels has not always been accepted with great enthusiasm by the church. To many people, if Jesus did not say what Scripture says he did, then Scripture is false and Christian faith is a sham. If Jesus did not actually say "I am the way, and the truth, and the life" (John 14:6), as Scripture reports, then he is not, and that statement is a falsehood. Such an approach, however, does not understand that Scripture is proclamation and not biography and that there are different ways in which a statement can be true. From the perspective of Christian faith, the claim that Jesus is the way, the truth, and the life is true regardless of whether Jesus uttered those words. That claim represents the true identity of Jesus of Nazareth from the perspective of Easter faith. That Jesus made that claim about himself neither adds to nor detracts from the truth of the statement. In the context of the Easter faith of the early Christian community, that claim is true regardless of what Jesus said about himself.

Because of the confessional nature of the Gospels, we cannot interrogate them in the same way that we would biographies or other documents that are intended to be read as history. That does not mean, however, that no historical questions can be asked of the New Testament. A central feature of the Gospels and of Christian faith is that their primary referent is the historical figure, Jesus of Nazareth. Questions about Christian faith begin with the historical Jesus and Scripture's witness to him. And it is precisely because Christian faith begins here—with the Jesus of the New Testament—that Christians cannot avoid the difficult task of historical inquiry.

Because of what some Christians believe about the resurrection, for example, the discovery of a tomb and a skeleton in Jerusalem, a tomb which could be shown to be that of Jesus of Nazareth, would destroy their Christian faith. For other Christians, no historical discovery could shake the foundations of faith.

Although Scripture may not answer all or even most of the questions we ask about the historical Jesus, it does tell us some important things about him. The very nature of Scripture as a confessional message for a preaching church means that we cannot reconstruct a biography of Jesus from the Gospels. But in Scripture's witness to Jesus as the Christ we are given some significant information about the historical figure who stands at the center of the story.

THE JESUS OF THE GOSPELS

If we attempt to find the historical Jesus in the midst of the Gospels' witness to the risen Christ, a number of probable historical facts emerge. We have good reason to think that Jesus was born at the beginning of the first century, that his parents were named Mary and Joseph, that he was from Nazareth in Galilee, and that he probably spoke Aramaic, the language of that region. We know very little about Jesus' birth and youth prior to his baptism by John the Baptist. The stories that we have at the beginning of

Matthew and Luke (but not Mark and John) are the confession of the early church that the Jesus whom God raised from the dead was from the beginning the chosen one of God, the Messiah, the Christ.

Properly understood, the Gospels should be read backward, because they are written from the perspective of the church's Easter faith. When interpreted in this context, the birth and infancy stories in the Gospels are the response of the church to the question: Who was this Jesus whom God raised from the dead? The birth stories are the church's confession that from the very beginning Jesus was the presence of God's love and grace in the world. Twentieth-century Christians often misunderstand the "miracle" of Jesus' birth. The miracle has nothing to do with how Jesus was conceived, that is, whether he was an instance of parthenogenesis, or virgin birth. The miracle that the Christmas stories celebrate is that the man Jesus was from the beginning the presence of the reality of God's love in the world.

The opening chapters of Matthew and Luke do point, however, to one historical fact that is of great importance for understanding who Jesus is. The New Testament leaves no doubt that Jesus was Jewish. The first chapter of Matthew traces Jesus' genealogy from Abraham through David to Joseph and Mary. The third chapter of Luke (3:23–38) traces Jesus' lineage from Joseph back to Adam. The genealogies, especially Matthew's, insist that, in order to understand the identity of Jesus of Nazareth, one must know him in the context of the history of Israel. Christians believe that all the promises of God come to fruition in Jesus of Nazareth. That is only one reason why the Christian community has insisted that the New Testament and the Hebrew Scriptures make up one canon and that the latter should never be removed from the Bible. The church has long recognized that without the Hebrew Scriptures it would not fully be able to understand the

New Testament confession that Jesus is the Christ.

For various reasons, Christians have not always been able to acknowledge Jesus' Jewishness. In some of the more sordid periods of the church's history, attempts were made to deny Jesus' Jewishness, but the evidence in the New Testament makes that impossible. Scripture clearly affirms that Jesus is a child of Israel. Theologically, of course, it is important to affirm Jesus' Jewishness if continuity is to be maintained between the Old and the New Testament. There are, however, other reasons for affirming Jesus' Jewishness which are equally important. If we are to understand what the New Testament presents as the teaching and ministry of Jesus, then we must approach Jesus in the context of his Jewish heritage. Christians have many things they want to say about Jesus, but one of those must be that Jesus was a devout Jew. Unless the Jesus of the Gospels is understood in his relation to the faith of Israel, then much of what the New Testament proclaims about him will be misinterpreted or unintelligible.

The claim that Jesus was a devout Jew does not mean that Jesus wholly accepted the interpretations and applications of Jewish faith in his day. Clearly he did not. Much of the Gospels is devoted to the continuing controversy between Jesus and established Jewish groups, such as the Pharisees and the Sadducees. A central point in this dispute is what Jesus had to say about Jewish law. On the one hand, he affirms the importance and abiding validity of the law. The Gospels report him as saying: "Think not that I have come to abolish the law and the prophets; I have come not to abolish them but to fulfil them" (Matt. 5:17). In response to a scribe's question about which is the first of the commandments (Mark 12:28–31), Jesus quotes Deut. 6:4–5, and Lev. 19:18, saying that one should love God with all one's heart, soul, mind, and strength, and should love one's neighbor as oneself. In numerous other contexts, Jesus affirms the validity of the law, yet he also demonstrates a remarkable freedom in relation to the law. In a variety of situations, Jesus insists that the law is not an end in itself but must be understood in relation to the love of God. When confronted by the Pharisees with a woman caught in adultery, who according to Jewish law should be stoned, Jesus responds, "Let him who is without sin among you be the first to throw a stone at her" (John 8:7). When Jesus enters a synagogue on the Sabbath and encounters a man with a withered hand, he does not hesitate to heal him, even in the presence of the Pharisees and even though such an act violates Sabbath law. Jesus asks the Pharisees, "Is it lawful on the sabbath to do good or to do harm, to save life or to kill?" (Mark 3:4).

An indication of the way in which Jesus both affirms and yet transcends Jewish law is the remarkable authority he exercises. Israel had known many prophets who came with the Word of the Lord on their lips. The prophets of the Old Testament prefaced what they had to say to the people of Israel with the words, "Thus says the LORD." Jesus, however, does not preface his sayings with these familiar words of prophetic address. Furthermore, he claims an authority to interpret the law. In the Sermon on the Mount (Matthew 5–7), Jesus says, "You have heard that it was said to the men of old" (Matt. 5:21), and then quotes the commandments concerning murder, adultery, divorce, false swearing, vengeance, and treatment of neighbors. After rehearsing these familiar commandments of the law, Jesus then says something very strange. He says, "But I say to you":

> You have heard that it was said, "An eye for an eye and a tooth for a tooth." But I say to you, Do not resist one who is evil. (Matt. 5:38–39)

Jesus does not deny the validity of the law, but he insists that the law must be understood and practiced in the broader context of God's grace and love. What he says is authoritative because he says it: "But I say to you." The authority of Jesus' words has something to do with who Jesus is and what he does.

The New Testament makes it very clear that Jesus is not merely one of Israel's prophets. That point is demonstrated by another unusual feature of the Gospel narratives. Jesus refers to God in the Gospels in a way that traditional Judaism did not. In Mark's description of Jesus in Gethsemane, for example, Jesus prays:

> Abba, Father, all things are possible to thee; remove this cup from me; yet not what I will, but what thou wilt. (Mark 14:36)

The expression "Abba" is one of deep intimacy, the most familiar and affectionate language a child could use in addressing a parent. Traditional Judaism emphasized the majesty and holiness of Yahweh, and would have found it unthinkable (and probably blasphemous) to use so intimate a term in language addressed to God. Furthermore, not only does Jesus dare to speak to God in such intimate language; he also teaches his followers and disciples to address God as "Father." The prayer that Jesus teaches his disciples begins, "Father, hallowed be thy name" (Luke 11:2). The New Testament scholar Eduard Schweizer sums up the implications of Jesus' use of the term "Abba":

> What is new is not that Jesus taught men to call God "Father"; it is that a people more sensitive than any other to the distance between God and man, between God and the world, were granted the freedom to say "Abba."

Jesus' freedom both in his use of the law and in his use of the term "Abba" demonstrates that he exercises a remarkable (and, to some people, perhaps offensive) authority in what he says and does.

Because of the confessional nature of the New Testament we do not know what Jesus thought about himself or whether he knew himself to be the Christ or the Messiah.

We do know, however, that after his baptism by John the Baptist, Jesus conducted a brief ministry of perhaps a year or more in Palestine. In his ministry Jesus taught primarily by means of parables, and most of Jesus' parables were devoted to a single theme—the coming kingdom of God. A single verse in the first chapter of Mark's Gospel summarizes the content of Jesus' teaching and preaching: "The time is fulfilled, and the kingdom of God is at hand; repent, and believe in the gospel" (Mark 1:15). At the center of Jesus' teaching, healing, and preaching is the symbol of the kingdom of God, and Jesus' parables communicate something of the power and nature of that kingdom.

Jesus' preaching and teaching do not focus primarily on a new form of morality. Nor does Jesus seem primarily concerned with teaching new religious beliefs. One reality dominates Jesus' teaching and ministry—repentance in preparation for the coming of God's kingdom. If one reads through the Gospels, the centrality of the kingdom of God in Jesus' teaching and preaching is obvious—so obvious that it is difficult to understand how so many of those who have searched the New Testament for a historical Jesus could have missed it. Many of the portraits of Jesus that have emerged in the nineteenth and twentieth centuries describe a teacher of morality or a great psychologist and spiritual leader. These portraits, however, have little to do with the Jesus described in the Gospels. The gospel that Jesus preaches does indeed have significant implications for morality, psychological health, and spiritual peace, but these are products of his emphasis on the central reality of the kingdom.

Four features of Jesus' teaching and preaching about God's coming kingdom are particularly important for understanding what the Gospels have to say about him. In the first place, it is important that Jesus speaks of the coming kingdom of God by means of parables. Jesus does not say, "The kingdom of God is this," or "The kingdom of

God is that." He says, "The kingdom of God is like," and then tells a parable.

> The kingdom of heaven is like leaven which a woman took and hid in three measures of flour, till it was all leavened. (Matt. 13:33)

Why did Jesus teach in parables? That question cannot be answered conclusively, but given the content of Jesus' parables, it seems likely that the nature of the kingdom (and therein the nature of its Lord) is such that it cannot be described in objective, factual terms. The kingdom of God is what is ultimately real, but it is hidden in what the world believes to be real, even though what the world considers real is only apparent. Jesus clearly intends his parables to evoke a response of repentance, conversion, and transformation. Because the parables are a form of metaphor, they enable those who hear them to identify with the familiar and be drawn into the world of the parable. But when people enter the parable's world they also encounter the hidden, the unexpected, and may be transformed by it.

Secondly, Jesus' parables turn the familiar world upside down. What is considered reality in the familiar world is transformed in God's kingdom. In the familiar world one gets what one deserves, or at least one should. In God's kingdom, however, the miracle of grace replaces the "just deserts" of merit. In Jesus' parable of the laborers in the vineyard (Matt. 20:1–16), all the workers are paid the same, regardless of how long they worked in the vineyard. Those who worked all day are paid the same as those who arrived at the eleventh hour. Even worse, those who worked all day are forced to wait, while those who came late are paid first. When those hired early in the day grumble about the unfairness of the situation, the owner of the vineyard replies, "Am I not allowed to do what I choose with what belongs to me? Or do you begrudge my generosity?" And Jesus adds the words, "So the last will be first, and the first last" (Matt. 20:16).

Jesus' vision of the kingdom and discipleship turns upside down the commonly accepted values of the world. In Mark's Gospel, Jesus makes this claim explicit without using parables:

> If any man would come after me, let him deny himself and take up his cross and follow me. For whoever would save his life will lose it; and whoever loses his life for my sake and the gospel's will save it. (Mark 8:34–35)

The nature of God's coming kingdom and the discipleship to which Jesus calls his followers are characterized by the reign of God's grace and by self-denial on the part of those who participate in the kingdom.

Thirdly, there are many passages in the Gospels which suggest that Jesus understood the coming kingdom of God to be tied to his ministry and perhaps to his person. Some texts in the Gospels seem to suggest that a decision for or against Jesus is also a decision for or against the kingdom of God. In his instructions to his twelve disciples, Jesus says, "And you will be hated by all for my name's sake" (Matt. 10:22). And when John's disciples ask Jesus whether he is the Messiah, the one who is to come, Jesus tells them to report to John what they have seen—"the blind receive their sight, the lame walk, lepers are cleansed, and the deaf hear, the dead are raised up, the poor have good news preached to them" (Luke 7:22). Jesus adds, "And blessed is he who takes no offense at me." In Jesus' teaching there is indeed some evidence that he believed the kingdom of God to be appearing in the world in the midst of his ministry.

Not only does Jesus teach about the kingdom of God by means of parables; the Gospels, written from the perspective of the church's faith, suggest that Jesus himself is *the* parable of God's kingdom of love and grace. It is important to recognize that the Gospels are not just a series of parables or sayings of Jesus. The parables of the kingdom are presented in the framework of the Gospel narratives about Jesus' teaching and ministry, and without this larger framework, Jesus' parables would be open to misinterpretation. Jesus' parables must be understood in relation to the Gospels' description of what Jesus does. The one clarifies the other. Not only does Jesus teach about a kingdom of love and grace; he enacts the reality of that kingdom in his own life and ministry. Not only does Jesus suggest that those who are "last" in the social order will be "first" in God's kingdom; in his own ministry he seeks out the refuse of society—the lepers, the maimed, the tax collectors, the prostitutes—as special recipients of God's grace and love. He calls his disciples (and, through the Gospels, the church) to do the same. From the perspective of the church's Easter faith, Jesus of Nazareth is *the* parable of God's kingdom.

Finally, according to the Gospels, Jesus apparently believed that the kingdom of God was either appearing in the world in the midst of his ministry or at least was a reality that would appear very soon. Jesus' words and actions suggest that he believed God's kingdom hovered on the horizon. In his instructions to his disciples in Matthew 10, Jesus tells them to flee to another town when they are persecuted, "for truly, I say to you, you will not have gone through all the towns of Israel before the Son of man comes" (Matt. 10:23). And in Mark's Gospel, Jesus concludes his discussion of the meaning of discipleship by saying, "Truly, I say to you, there are some standing here who will not taste death before they see that the kingdom of God has come with power" (Mark 9:1).

Jesus' claims concerning the nearness of the kingdom posed serious difficulties for the church. There is some evidence in the New Testament that the earliest Christian communities, those formed soon after the Easter appearances, expected the kingdom to come very soon, only now they associated the coming of that kingdom with the return of Jesus. In some of his earliest letters, for example, Paul seems to believe that the return of Christ will take place soon. To the Christians at Thessalonica, Paul wrote:

> And the dead in Christ will rise first; then we who are alive, who are left, shall be caught up together with them in the clouds to meet the Lord in the air; and so we shall always be with the Lord. (I Thess. 4:16–17)

A major problem for the faith of the church was the fact that Jesus did not return, at least not in the way that was expected. The Christian community has dealt with that fact in various ways. Often it simply has ignored Jesus' teaching that the kingdom is coming soon. Another approach has been to spiritualize Jesus' message and insist that the kingdom Jesus was talking about is the inner peace of the gospel. Such interpretations appeal mistakenly to texts like Luke 17:21, in which Jesus says "for behold, the kingdom of God is in the midst of you." In either case, what the Gospels report as the teaching of Jesus is seriously distorted.

It was perhaps Jesus' sense of the nearness of the kingdom that led him to carry his teaching and his ministry to Jerusalem. Whatever Jesus' motives were, this decision was a fatal one. The journey to Jerusalem soon led him into conflict with the religious and political authorities of his day. Jesus was arrested, tried by the Jewish authorities, and turned over to the Roman government for punishment. The "passion" of Jesus—those events surrounding his trial and execution—receives considerable attention in the Gospels. Indeed, the "plot" of the Gospels builds in intensity as we approach the cross and resurrection. That Jesus of Nazareth was executed by crucifixion is perhaps the most reliable historical fact in the Gospels. While Jesus' execution on the cross may be indisputable, the Gospel accounts of his arrest, trial, and execution do not answer many of the historical questions we would like to ask. It is unclear, for example, precisely what the charges were against Jesus. There is some evidence in the Gospels (Mark 14:64 and Matt. 26:65) that Jesus was charged with blasphemy, but the appropriate form of punishment in Israel for blasphemy was stoning and not crucifixion. It is also unclear why the Gospels' description of Jesus' trial by the Sanhedrin violates so many established procedures of Jewish law. The events surrounding his arrest, trial, and execution are shrouded in mystery.

We do know that Jesus suffered an extremely painful form of death. Furthermore, we know that, according to Roman law, death on the cross was reserved only for the most serious of crimes—treason or attempts to overthrow the state and runaway slaves. When Jesus was executed, a sign, declaring his crime, was hung on this cross: "And the inscription of the charge against him read, 'The King of the Jews' " (Mark 15:26). The inscription on the cross may be the clearest indication we have of the charges against Jesus. Regardless of whether the charge was just, Jesus may have been executed because he was understood to be a troublemaker and a threat to established political and religious authority. That may not be how Jesus understood himself or his ministry, but it may be how he was understood by the political and religious establishment of his day.

Furthermore, the Gospels' descriptions of Jesus' death reflect the Christian conviction that Jesus' death is not only the death of a good man but also the overcoming of the sin that separates God from the world. The Gospels point to that fact by recording that when Jesus died, the curtain in the Temple, which veiled God's presence, was torn in two from top to bottom. With the death of Jesus, nothing stands between God and humanity, except Jesus the Mediator.

Finally, the Gospels tell us that a strange thing happened after Jesus' death. Soon after his death, many of Jesus' disciples gathered again in Jerusalem and told stories about the crucified Jesus having appeared to them. His disciples proclaimed that the crucified Jesus had been raised from the dead by God and that he was indeed the Christ, the long-awaited one, who would destroy the demonic powers, including death itself. These Easter encounters with the risen Jesus prompted the church's confession, "Jesus is Lord." Filled with this faith and inspired by their experience of the abiding presence of Jesus, early Christian communities soon began to proclaim their "good news" to the rest of the world. The Jesus who had proclaimed the kingdom now became the one proclaimed and the very meaning of the kingdom itself.

JESUS' TITLES

The Gospel narratives are not the only way that Scripture proclaims who Jesus is. They are certainly the primary way, but in addition the New Testament has another way of identifying Jesus—by means of titles. Jesus is given many different titles in the New Testament, and each title provides him a form of identity. Some of the most frequent and important titles he is given are the Christ *(Christos)*, the Messiah, Son of David, Suffering Servant, Son of Man, our High Priest, the Son of God, Savior, and Lord *(Kyrios)*. Each of these titles makes a distinctive claim about Jesus' identity, and each of them must be understood in the historical context of Jewish and Greek thought during the first century.

In any discussion of the titles given to Jesus in the New Testament, two basic points must be examined. The first concerns the use of some or all of the titles by Jesus of Nazareth and his understanding of their meaning. Did Jesus refer to himself as the Messiah or the Son of God, and did he mean by those titles what the Easter church meant when it attributed them to him? That question is yet another example of an important historical question which we cannot answer with certainty on the basis of the evidence in the New Testament. The best New Testament scholarship suggests that it is unlikely that Jesus referred to himself as either Messiah or Son of God. These are titles which the Easter church, living on this side of the resurrection, attributes to Jesus in order to confess its faith in him. The church puts these titles in Jesus' mouth in order to make its identification of him explicit. As far as the early church was concerned, Jesus was indeed the Messiah and the Son of God regardless of whether he made such a claim for himself. The church's experience with the risen Jesus enabled it to identify him as Messiah and Son of God, not its recollections about what Jesus said about himself.

Part of the problem, as we noted previously, is that the New Testament does not give us reliable historical material for determining what Jesus thought about himself. Nor does the New Testament give us the necessary evidence to determine whether Jesus actually used the titles the writers of the New Testament attributed to him, and, if he did, what he meant by them. The title "Son of man" is a case in point. "Son of man" was not a title invented by Jesus or by the early church. It is a term that can be found in the literature of Jewish apocalyptic (writings which look forward to the end of history and the triumph of God), for example in Dan. 7:13ff., and it refers to that figure who will end the present age and inaugurate a new heaven and a new earth. In the Gospels, Jesus sometimes appears to use the term "Son of man" in reference to himself, as in Matt. 8:20, "Foxes have holes, and birds of the air have nests; but the Son of man has nowhere to lay his head." In other texts, however, Jesus appears to refer to a Son of man who is not to be identified with himself, as in Luke 12:8ff., "And I tell you, every one who acknowledges me before men, the Son of man also will acknowledge before the angels of God." If those texts which speak of the Son of man in the future tense are more likely authentic words of Jesus than those which speak of him in the present, then it seems clear that while the church used the title "Son of man" to identify Jesus, it is unlikely that Jesus used the title in reference to himself.

A second consideration concerns the meaning of the titles given to Christ. It is not the case that the church simply took familiar titles, such as Messiah and Suffering Servant, applied them to Jesus, and in so doing gave Jesus his true identity. On the contrary, the relation between Jesus and these titles is more complex than that. Most of the titles do have familiar connotations in Greek and Jewish contexts, but the New Testament does not simply apply these titles with their original meaning to Jesus of Nazareth. In practically every case, the titles are redefined by the Gospel narratives about Jesus. The titles are given a new meaning in the light of what the Gospels report about Jesus. They do not entirely lose their original meaning, but are reworked in the context of the Gospel narratives. That major development is particularly apparent in the Gospels' use of one of the most important titles—Son of God.

The Gospel of Mark is especially concerned with the proper interpretation of the title "Son of God" and what it means to attribute the title to Jesus. Prior to the final events of Mark's Gospel, no figure is allowed to refer to Jesus as Son of God and go unrebuked by him except the demons. In Mark's Gospel, the demons apparently know who Jesus is and what it means to call him Son of God, while everyone else surrounding Jesus does not.

And whenever the unclean spirits beheld him, they fell down before him and cried out, "You are the Son of God." And he strictly ordered them not to make him known. (Mark 3:11–12)

Neither Jesus' disciples nor his family recognize who he truly is. The most obvious example of this "blindness" is Peter's response to Jesus at Caesarea Philippi (Mark 8: 27–33). Jesus asks his disciples (and through Mark's Gospel those of us who are its readers), "Who do you say that I am?" And Peter apparently answers correctly, "You are the Christ." But when Jesus then tells his disciples that he "must suffer many things" and be killed, Peter rebukes him. Clearly what Peter means by the title "Christ" is not what Jesus meant. And the incident closes with Jesus' angry words to Peter: "Get behind me, Satan! For you are not on the side of God, but of men."

In Mark's Gospel, the only person who is permitted to call Jesus the Son of God and not be rebuked is the Roman centurion at the crucifixion. Mark allows the centurion to say, "Truly this man was the Son of God" (Mark 15:39), but only because the centurion stands face-to-face with the crucified Jesus. Mark's point is obvious. What it means to say that Jesus is the Son of God is to know him as the crucified Christ.

All of the titles the New Testament uses to give Jesus his true identity, including Christ and Son of God, have their proper meaning in the narratives that make up the Gospels. In order to know what the titles mean, it is important to know something of their original meaning and their historical development. At the same time, each of the titles must also be understood in relation to the Gospel narratives about Jesus. And what is true of the New Testament titles is also true of the other things that the chruch has wanted to confess about Jesus. The church's claims about Jesus must always be examined in their relation to the Jesus of the Scriptures. In order to assess the adequacy of its confessions about Jesus, the church has always found itself forced to reexamine Scripture's descriptions of him.

3
THE CHRIST OF THE CHURCH

The question of the true identity of Jesus of Nazareth, as we saw in Chapter 2, is a central concern of the New Testament. It is not surprising, therefore, that Christian communities, who understand faith and life by means of Scripture, also have had to deal with the question of Jesus' identity. A significant part of the life and thought of the Christian church has been devoted to Bonhoeffer's question, "Who is Jesus Christ for us today?"

As the Christian community found itself facing new problems concerning the meaning of faith, it discovered that it could not simply repeat Scripture as an adequate answer to the situation. It turned to Scripture for guidance, but it also found it had to reinterpret the gospel in each new situation. Consequently, at different points in history the church developed new forms of language and new creeds and confessions, in addition to those in Scripture, in order to make clear its understanding of the gospel.

WHY CREEDS?

In the first five centuries of the Christian era, there were numerous disagreements in the church about the true identity of Jesus of Nazareth. To many people today, those historical arguments sound tedious and unnecessary. It is not always clear why these subtle theological debates were significant for the life of the church.

Some of these arguments about Jesus during the fourth and fifth centuries were indeed carried on at a very sophisticated level. Church politics often did play a very important role in determining the outcome of the debates. Still, these theological controversies about the sense in which Jesus is and is not the Christ, the chosen one of God, were of significance not only to theologians but to the whole church. The reason the church expended such enormous amounts of time and intellectual energy in its debates about Jesus is that the stakes were high—nothing less than the meaning of salvation. No matter how obscure the early church's debates about Jesus may sound, in almost every case what fueled the fire was a genuine concern on all sides that Christian faith not be misrepresented and salvation not be misinterpreted.

Secondly, what strikes the modern reader as a major weakness of the early church's creeds—their archaic language—actually may be their greatest strength. There is no such thing as a "timeless" creed, one that is written for all times and situations. The church's creeds, like its Scriptures, were written at particular points in history in response to specific issues in the interpretation of Christian faith and discipleship. In order to answer those issues responsibly, the church found itself compelled to articulate its faith in the language of the culture it was addressing. In the fourth and fifth centuries the dominant cultures were Greek and Roman, and, not surprisingly, the church formulated its confessions about Jesus in the language of those cultures. Although terms such as "substance" and "nature" may sound strange to us when applied to Jesus, they were not strange to the fifth century. It may be that the modern church will have to develop its own language and imagery to express its claim that Jesus is the Christ, but it cannot do that simply by repeating the creeds of the early church. At the same time, if the church is to avoid the mistakes and blind alleys it encountered in the past, it must listen to the early church's creeds and confessions and be instructed by them.

In the church's first five centuries, there were many discussions of Jesus' relation to God and the sense in which Jesus is the Christ. We cannot possibly review all of them here. (J. N. D. Kelly's *Early Christian Doctrines* provides a good summary.) But it is important that we review the major issues and figures in these debates.

Every Christological discussion of Jesus is crucial because Christians believe that Jesus of Nazareth reveals the meaning and reality of salvation. Debates about Jesus are always also debates about the meaning of salvation. In even the most sophisticated Christological discussions, the issues are not just fine points of technical theology but basic issues that involve the meaning of the gospel.

At times the church has found it necessary to declare a particular interpretation of Christian faith and life unfaithful to the gospel of Jesus Christ. The judgment that a theological position is heresy is always just as tentative as the church's statements of faith. Both judgments are open to subsequent revision and correction. Yesterday's heresies have a way of becoming today's orthodoxy, and vice versa. But because of the negative connotations carried by the term "heresy," it is also important to note that practically every heretic in the history of the church has been *partially* correct. Practically every position the church has labeled heresy has possessed an element of what Christians understand to be the truth of faith. Often the position becomes heresy because it attempts to erect the entire edifice of faith upon only a partial truth.

Some Christians react cautiously and fearfully to the suggestion that the church may need something other than Scripture and the ancient creeds in order to articulate its faith. Caution in these matters is commendable, but fear is not. There is wisdom, tried by history, in the church's classical creeds, but any and every attempt at proclamation of the gospel involves interpretation. A faith that clings to the past and lives in fear of the new cannot be faithful to the gospel. But before we make any judgments about the adequacy of the church's classical creeds and before we raise the question of what new directions might be pursued today, it is necessary that we briefly review the basic language and content of the church's early Christology.

CLASSICAL CHRISTOLOGY

Almost from the beginning, the church's thinking about Jesus was cast between two ends of a spectrum. At one end of the spectrum was something called Docetism, and at the opposite end was a position called Ebionitism. The church rejected both of these positions, declared them to be heresy, and attempted to formulate its own confession somewhere between these two extremes.

The Ebionites were Jewish Christians in the second century who acknowledged Jesus to be the Messiah, but who insisted that Jesus was a fully human being and not the incarnate Word of God. We may surmise that one reason the Ebionites refused to confess the deity of Jesus is that their Jewish heritage would not allow them to affirm that Yahweh could be known in a person. Jewish Christians continued to confess that "The Lord is our God, the Lord alone" (Deut. 6:4), and any claim that Jesus was the very reality of God would have seemed to contradict the claim that God was one.

The other position was Docetism. The Docetists believed that Jesus of Nazareth was indeed God in the flesh, but that he was not really human. Though he appeared to be human, he was actually God in disguise. Because the

Docetists believed that Jesus was God and that God could not suffer, the agony of Jesus on the cross was in their eyes only apparent but not real. Jesus was God in the form of a human being but not actually a human being.

The church rejected the Docetists' claims about Jesus for the same reasons that it rejected those of the Ebionites. While the Ebionites denied that Jesus was anything other than fully human, the Docetists denied that Jesus was anything other than fully God. Both positions threatened the central Christian claim that salvation is God's activity of reconciliation, an activity that has become tangible in human history in the person of Jesus of Nazareth. By denying that in Jesus of Nazareth we encounter the very reality of God, the Ebionites could not say that Jesus is *God's* forgiveness and *God's* act of salvation. The new life offered the world in Jesus Christ may be that of a noble human example, but it was not something made possible by God. The Docetists, on the other hand, refused to acknowledge the full humanity of Jesus, and in so doing they were unable to say that God's act of forgiveness and salvation had actually taken place in the midst of human history, in one who was like us in every respect except sin.

For important and valid reasons the church rejected both Ebionitism and Docetism. Yet these two positions have never wholly disappeared from the church. Even today it is possible to discover varieties of each in the church. Those interpretations of Jesus which affirm that he was a man of unusual moral character, a great teacher and spiritual leader, perhaps the greatest of the world's prophets, are often a version of Ebionitism. Perhaps the most familiar contemporary form of Ebionitism is that which depicts Jesus as the great moral teacher. As in most cases of Ebionitism, the sayings of Jesus the moral teacher become more important than his person and the events that make up his life. The Sermon on the Mount becomes the center of the gospel, and the cross is nothing more than the tragic fate of a good man.

Any interpretation of Jesus Christ that denies his humanity is a form of Docetism and threatens the Christian understanding of salvation. There are many people in the church today who deny Jesus his humanity by insisting that he was omniscient and omnipotent. To be human is to exist within certain limitations of time and space, but Docetic interpretations of Jesus insist that he was not really confined to his culture and his setting in history, as are all other people. They argue that he did indeed know higher mathematics, modern physics, and the recent discoveries of modern science, that his uncertainty about the future was only a ruse, and that he knew precisely what the future held for him and for everyone else. The Docetists' Jesus is the world's greatest magician, capable of altering the probable laws of nature and performing stunts unmatched even in Hollywood. While the New Testament clearly reports that Jesus performed acts of healing and even exorcism, which evoked awe and wonder from those who witnessed them, those events are not the basis of the New Testament's confession that Jesus is Lord. While some of those events may indeed have been a part of Jesus' ministry, they are not the foundation of Christian faith. Other stories in Scripture, which attribute superhuman power to Jesus, must be understood in the context of the early church's faith. They point to the uniqueness and unrivaled authority of Jesus of Nazareth, and should be interpreted in that manner. They should not become the basis of claims that Jesus was either more or less than human. In the modern church, Docetism is probably more widespread than Ebionitism, but both should be combated just as vigorously now as they were in the early church.

Although the early church quickly understood that it could not affirm either Ebionitism or Docetism, it was slower to formulate the language for its own confession about Jesus Christ. In the fourth and fifth centuries, the church held a series of councils to hammer out acceptable language for its confession of faith. Two of these councils were especially important—Nicaea in A.D. 325 and Chalcedon in A.D. 451.

At the Council of Nicaea, the theological issue was not the relation between deity and humanity in Jesus, but the relation of Jesus to God. In other words, the issue at Nicaea was not so much Christology as it was the doctrine of the Trinity. This is significant because the modern church has discovered what the early church discovered. Without a doctrine of the Trinity important issues in Christology will remain confused and unresolved.

An example of the importance of the Trinity for the discussion of Christology was the recent furor in the Presbyterian church. A minister from another denomination received a call to co-pastor a Presbyterian church. When he was examined by the appropriate presbytery, he was asked whether he could affirm that Jesus is God. He responded, "Only God is God." That answer precipitated a heated debate in the Presbyterian church, a debate in which there was considerably more emotional heat than theological insight.

There is a sense, of course, in which the minister's response was both right and wrong. He was correct in that the New Testament does not say that God was Christ. It says that God was *in* Christ (II Cor. 5:19), and the preposition is terribly important in Christian theology. The church has indeed affirmed that Jesus and the Father are one (John 10:30), but it has also insisted that the Father and the Son should not be confused. The doctrine of the Trinity is the church's attempt to clarify that relation, and it is the Trinity that explains the sense in which Jesus is and is not God. Without the Trinity, the Christian confession that Jesus and the Father are one becomes hopelessly confusing. Unfortunately, what happened at Nicaea and what is meant by the confession that God is triune is rarely discussed or understood in most congregations. The Presbyterian church has recently reaped the harvest of that confusion.

At Nicaea the major issue was the relation between the Son or Word, incarnate in Jesus, and the Father. Was only the Father to be called God, or were both Father and Son to be referred to as God? If the latter, how was Christian faith not a form of polytheism (a belief in many gods)? Two major parties emerged and two formidable representatives: Arius and Athanasius. Those Christians who took Arius' side, much like the Ebionites, argued that God who is holy and transcendent could not be divisible. Because of God's majesty and uniqueness, it was inconceivable to the Arians that any being could share in God's nature.

To Christians who identified with Athanasius, Arius' views were wholly unacceptable and a clear threat to their understanding of salvation. Athanasius believed that it was precisely because the Son, who was truly God, had assumed real human flesh that salvation was a reality and human beings were no longer enslaved by sin. The Son and the Father were not the same individual, but they were of the same substance or essence. The Council of Nicaea sided with Athanasius against Arius, and it rejected each of the basic tenets of Arianism. It denied that the Son was created out of nothing, and it insisted that he was begotten of the Father before all worlds. Finally, and most important, the council affirmed that the Son is of the same substance with the Father, and, consequently, has the same attributes as the Father.

If one knows nothing of Arius and Athanasius and the issues that separated them, then it is possible to misread the Nicene Creed. The creed clearly affirms the deity of the Son, who was incarnate in Jesus of Nazareth. It does so, of course, because what was in question as a result of Arius' theology was the deity of the Son. No one doubted Jesus' humanity. However, the modern reader who interprets the Nicene Creed without knowledge of its historical context might conclude that the early church affirmed only the deity of Jesus Christ and said nothing about his humanity. Given the widespread Docetism in the modern church, there are good grounds for suspecting that many readers have come to that conclusion. Only if one knows the historical context in which the Nicene Creed was written will it be clear that the church had no intention of affirming the deity of the Son at the expense of Jesus' humanity.

The Council at Nicaea did not, however, answer all the questions about Jesus Christ. The Nicene Creed only stirred up the waters. In the fourth century, two major schools of Christological thought emerged during this period, one centered around Antioch and the other around Alexandria. The latter, the Alexandrian school, focused on the incarnation and began its theological reflection with the claim that Jesus Christ is one person in whom the incarnate Word dwells. This school is sometimes known as Word-flesh Christology, because it understood Jesus to be the incarnation of the Word in human flesh. Critics of this school worried that while it clearly affirmed the deity of Christ, stating that he was the Word incarnate, it failed to affirm his full humanity. In some versions of Word-flesh Christology, the Word appeared to replace Jesus' intellect or soul. Hence he was flesh, but he was not fully human because he was lacking a human soul or intellect.

The second major interpretation of Christ was centered at Antioch. The position that emerged from this school is sometimes known as Word-man Christology. The Antiochenes were troubled by the way in which the Alexandrians seemed to compromise Jesus' full humanity. The Antiochenes began with the claim that Jesus Christ was both fully human and the incarnation of the Word. They sought to protect the full humanity of Jesus by insisting that, like all other people, Jesus developed in his knowledge of the world and in his understanding of it.

The arguments between these two schools in the latter half of the fourth century and the first half of the fifth century became very bitter. At a series of councils and synods, the two sides took turns discovering extreme positions in the other camp which could be denounced as heresy. The differences between the Antiochenes and the Alexandrians were in part semantic. That is, the two schools were using different theological terms in their interpretations of Jesus Christ, and the terms they shared seemed to have different meanings in each school. By the first half of the fifth century, they had resolved their semantic differences. At Ephesus in 431 and at Chalcedon in 451, the church finally constructed language that was agreeable to many people in both camps. The Chalcedonian Decree became the church's classical statement about Jesus Christ. It affirmed that Jesus Christ is two natures in one person:

> the same perfect in Godhead, the same perfect in manhood, truly God and truly man, the same of a reasonable soul and body; consubstantial with the Father in Godhead, and the same consubstantial with us in manhood, like us in all things except sin; . . . acknowledged in two natures without confusion, without change, without division, without separation.

The statement acknowledged the Antiochene concern that Jesus' full humanity be protected. It affirmed both natures fully present in Jesus without either confusion or separation. And the statement acknowledged the Alexandrian concern that Jesus Christ not be divided, not be described as two Sons or persons rattling around in one human body. Chalcedon declared that in the one person Jesus, the world encounters the full reality of both true humanity and God.

Although controversy concerning the interpretation of Christ continued in the church, the Chalcedonian Decree became and remained for many centuries the center of the church's confession that Jesus is the Christ and that he and the Father are one. The church's two most important assertions were that the Son is of the same substance as the Father and that Jesus of Nazareth is both fully human and fully God, two natures in one person.

Occasionally, when one reads a summary of the early church's discussions of Christ, one gets the impression that the church's theologians did it a disservice by developing technical theological formulas. Such an impression of what the early church did is unfortunate. The leaders of the church who formulated the statements at Nicaea, Constantinople, Ephesus, and Chalcedon were acutely aware that they were dealing with a holy mystery—holy because it had something to do with God's redemption of humanity, and a mystery because it could not be fully explained or described by any theological formula. Yet they also recognized that, if the church intended to proclaim the gospel faithfully to the world, it must make its confession about Jesus Christ as clear and as intelligible as possible.

As we shall see, numerous questions have been raised inside and outside the church about the church's classic language about Jesus Christ. While some of us may find those questions compelling and may believe that the church must develop new language and imagery to make its confession that "God was in Christ," we should keep in mind that the church has not clung to the language of the fourth and fifth centuries simply out of stubbornness. It has continued to use that language because none other has been proposed which comes as close to the heart of the Christian mystery. As G. K. Chesterton (1874–1936) wrote many years ago:

> For orthodox theology has specially insisted that Christ was not a being apart from God and man, like an elf, nor yet a being half human and half not, like a centaur, but both things at once and both things thoroughly, very man and very God.

That is the divine mystery Christians believe about Jesus
Christ, and no human formula quite does it justice. The
Danish theologian Søren Kierkegaard (1813–1855) tried to
make the same point: "At every moment Christ is God just
as much as he is man—just as the sky seems to be as deep
in the sea as it is high above the sea." Or as a familiar hymn
puts it:

> I know not how that Bethlehem's Babe
> Could in the Godhead be;
> I only know the manger Child
> Has brought God's life to me.

CRITICISMS OF CLASSICAL CHRISTOLOGY

For many centuries the early church's language about
Christ was widely accepted. The major leaders of the Ref-
ormation, Martin Luther and John Calvin, readily affirmed
the language of Nicaea and Chalcedon. Beginning in the
Enlightenment, however, questions were raised about the
adequacy of the classical view of Christ. These questions
have been refined considerably in the nineteenth and
twentieth centuries and have forced all Christians, even
those in sympathy with the early church, to rethink the
issues in the ancient creeds. Of the many questions that
have been raised about classical Christology, four are particularly important.

First, many theologians have asked whether the classical view of Christ makes sense to twentieth-century Christians. As we already have observed, no creed or confession
is timeless or authoritative for every age. Every creed is
addressed to particular questions that have arisen at a
given point in history. A good creed addresses those questions in language that is clear and meaningful to those who
posed the questions. Classical Christology uses terms that
were meaningful to Greek and Roman culture of the
fourth and fifth centuries, terms such as substance, es-

sence, and nature. But those terms may no longer be meaningful to Christians living in the twentieth century. If we could survey all the Christians who recite the confession that Jesus Christ is "of one substance with the Father" in their Sunday worship services, we would probably be alarmed at how few understand what they are confessing.

Part of the problem is that we no longer understand anthropology or human nature the same way as did people in the fourth and fifth centuries. Terms such as "substance" and "nature" were familiar and appropriate in the fourth century, but we no longer understand human identity by means of those terms. The modern Christian cannot invoke fifth-century categories to describe the identity of Jesus of Nazareth without running the high risk of being seriously misunderstood or simply ignored. As far as some theologians are concerned, that does not mean that the church should discard its classical creeds. They always serve as guides and instructors to the church. But the church must formulate new language by which to make the same confession as the fifth-century church did, new language which will be intelligible to people living in the twentieth century. Much of modern theological discussion about Jesus Christ has been devoted to that effort.

Second, in addition to the problem of interpretation, many modern theologians have been troubled by the focus of classical Christology. In both the Nicene Creed and the Chalcedonian Decree, the emphasis falls heavily on the incarnation, the claim that in Jesus of Nazareth the Word became flesh. Very little is said in either creed, however, about the rest of Jesus' life. His teaching and ministry are not even mentioned. We have discussed some of the historical reasons for the creeds' emphasis on the incarnation, but many contemporary Christians worry about the creeds' silence concerning Jesus between incarnation and passion.

Some Christians, for example, think that the early

church has reversed the structure of New Testament faith. While classical Christology seems to emphasize Christmas and Bethlehem, the New Testament begins with Golgotha and Easter and looks backward from the perspective of its Easter faith. Both Christmas and Easter are necessary for a full appreciation of Christian faith, but in the experience of the early church it was Easter and not Christmas that was the foundation of Christian faith. It was Easter that raised the question, Who was this Jew that God raised from the dead? The incarnation and the church's Christmas stories are its answer to that question, its affirmation that from the very beginning this Jesus was the reality of God present in the world. But without the church's experience of Easter and the faith it evoked, there would have been no questions about incarnation and no Christian faith. The apostle Paul has a great deal to say about Jesus' resurrection, but virtually nothing to say about the incarnation.

Third, one consequence of the emphasis on incarnation in classical Christology is that it seems to deemphasize the full humanity of Jesus of Nazareth. The Nicene Creed does indeed affirm that Jesus Christ "was made man," but that is the only point at which it dips briefly into the full reality of human history. The major pillars of this creed stand on either side of this brief phrase—incarnation on the one side, and passion and resurrection on the other. As we have noted several times, when the Nicene Creed is interpreted in its historical context, its emphasis on the incarnation and resurrection is understandable. When taken out of that historical context, however, the creed could be interpreted as affirming the deity and ignoring the full humanity—the teaching, ministry, and deeds—of Jesus. If taken to an extreme position, such an interpretation could lead to a form of Docetism, in which Jesus' humanity is either ignored or denied.

That misinterpretation should not occur if the creed is understood in its historical context, and, most important, in relation to Scripture. The New Testament Gospels do not rush from Bethlehem to Easter. On the contrary, they linger considerably over important incidents in Jesus' teaching and ministry, as if they were trying to tell us that neither Bethlehem nor Easter can be understood properly unless they are interpreted in the context of the whole gospel, the whole account of the man from Nazareth who proclaimed the gospel and ate and drank with the outcasts of society, as though the last were indeed first and the first last.

Finally, giving little attention to the teaching and ministry of Jesus may endanger an important principle in Christian theology. Christian theology has long claimed that who Jesus is cannot be separated from what he did. Also, it has insisted that what Jesus said (his teaching) cannot and should not be separated from how he lived (his ministry). When Christians confess that Jesus was fully human but without sin (Heb. 4:15), part of what they mean is that Jesus is unlike every other sinful person; there is no conflict between who Jesus is and what he does. The apostle Paul articulates the universal human experience of sin when he writes, "For I do not do the good I want, but the evil I do not want is what I do" (Rom. 7:19). In Jesus, on the other hand, Christians believe they see the perfect combination of intention and action, of person and work.

This theological principle is an important corollary of the Christian claim that Jesus defines the meaning of salvation. The incarnation, taken in isolation, is not a statement of Christian faith. According to the New Testament, the basis of salvation is not simply that the Word became flesh, but that the Word became flesh in Jesus of Nazareth. The Gospels' descriptions of Jesus of Nazareth give flesh-and-blood meaning to our understanding of salvation. In order to understand what it means when it speaks of love and reconciliation, the New Testament directs our attention to its picture of the teaching, ministry, and death of Jesus.

Furthermore, we also noted in Chapter 1 that the identity of individual Christians, as well as the identity of the Christian community, is shaped by Jesus of Nazareth. Christian faith is not only something that is believed but also something that is lived, and the living of it is what the New Testament refers to as discipleship. Christian individuals and communities try to live in the world in faithful obedience to the grace of God as they believe they have seen and known it in Jesus of Nazareth. Although Christian discipleship can never be simply a matter of repeating what Jesus said or did in specific situations, Christians do believe that the question of what discipleship means in any situation is informed by the New Testament's descriptions of the teaching and ministry of Jesus.

Yet another implication of the unity of the person and work of Jesus, as we are reminded by *The Documents of Vatican II,* is the claim that theology cannot be separated from ethics.

> He worked with human hands, He thought with a human mind, acted by human choice, and loved with a human heart. Born of the Virgin Mary, He has truly been made one of us, like us in all things except sin.

We see the same concern for both the deity and the humanity of Jesus expressed in some of the most recent Presbyterian confessions. In the Confession of 1967, the most recent confession of The United Presbyterian Church in the United States of America, the major theological theme is reconciliation. That confession attempts to present the meaning of Christian faith and discipleship for a church facing specific social issues in the twentieth century. In response to issues such as racism, war, poverty, and sexual relationships, the confession points to the New Testament theme of reconciliation. But the confession's discussion of what reconciliation means for these specific issues is prefaced by a look at God's work of reconciliation in Jesus Christ. In this context the confession declares that in Jesus "true humanity was realized once for all." What reconciliation means for difficult contemporary social issues, such as racism and world peace, can be discovered only by looking first at the one specific picture that Christians have of reconciliation, and that of course is the reconciliation taught and embodied by Jesus and vindicated by God in Jesus' resurrection.

The Presbyterian Church in the United States recently considered a contemporary confession entitled "A Declaration of Faith." Like the Confession of 1967, the Declaration places greater emphasis on the humanity of Jesus than did some of the classical confessions:

> Jesus was what we are,
> He grew up in a family and a society
>   troubled by the common problems of the world.
> His knowledge was limited
>   by his time and place in history.
> He felt deeply the joy of friendship
>   and the hurt of being rejected.
> Jesus prayed,
>   struggled with temptation,
>   knew anger,
>   and was subject to suffering and death.
> He was like us in every way except sin.

The Declaration of Faith emphasizes Jesus' healing and teaching, and it links the mission of the church to Jesus' ministry. At the same time, it does not ignore the central claims of the classical creeds. The Declaration stands in the same tradition as Nicaea and Chalcedon when it affirms that in Jesus of Nazareth the world encounters the reality of God:

> In the person and work of Jesus,
>   God himself and a human life
>   are united but not confused,
>   distinguished but not separated.
> The coming of Jesus was itself

the coming of God's promised rule.
Through his birth, life, death, and resurrection,
    he brings about the relationship between God
    and humanity
    that God always intended.

4
JESUS AND THE THEOLOGIANS

For the past two hundred years, theologians have been searching for language that will enable the church to confess its faith in the Lordship of Jesus Christ and to make its confession intelligible to contemporary culture. In most cases, theologians have not simply turned their backs on the church's classical creeds and confessions. They have been guided and instructed by that confessional heritage, and have attempted to avoid the mistakes and pitfalls which the early creeds rejected. Modern theologians share with their sisters and brothers in the early church a common confession of the Lordship of Jesus Christ, but they also recognize, as did their predecessors, the importance of making the church's confessions about Jesus Christ come alive for the culture in which they live. Consequently, they have sought to develop language and imagery that will honor the common faith of the church through the ages and yet speak clearly and meaningfully to the contemporary world.

Of course, the search for new language about Christ has been something more than an exercise in translation. Modern theologians have not simply developed new terms for the translation of traditional doctrines. In developing new language for the church to confess its faith, theologians have also altered the meaning of some traditional doctrines. In most cases, however, theologians have not invented these new meanings. The development of new idioms and the reinterpretation of Christian faith by modern theology only reflect the contemporary church's ever-new experience of God's grace and the meaning of the gospel. Modern theologians have merely responded to the church's changing experience of God's grace and its new understanding of the gospel. In this chapter we will survey briefly a few of the proposals that have been made in contemporary theology for the reinterpretation of the church's confession of the Lordship of Jesus Christ.

CONTEMPORARY INTERPRETATIONS OF JESUS

Almost every new theological proposal in the last two hundred years has included reinterpretation of Christology. Because Jesus Christ is the center of Christian faith, the reinterpretation of Christian theology usually has begun with a rethinking of the church's understanding of Jesus Christ. We cannot examine all the reinterpretations of Jesus Christ that have appeared in modern theology, but four basic types of Christology have dominated the contemporary discussion. These four types of modern Christology focus on Jesus' God-consciousness, Jesus and the experience of salvation, Jesus the liberator, and Jesus' openness to God.

The first major Christological proposal in the modern period, and still one of the most important, was that of Friedrich Schleiermacher (1768–1834). In *The Christian Faith*, published in 1821–22 and revised in 1830–31, Schleiermacher departed from the categories of classical Christology and developed an interpretation of Jesus as the Christ in terms of his perfect God-consciousness. As Schleiermacher described him, Jesus was the mediator of the experience of redemption in the Christian community, but Jesus functioned that way because his sensible consciousness was determined at every moment by a perfect God-consciousness, an awareness of his relation to God undistorted by human sin. Schleiermacher believed that Jesus' perfect God-consciousness did develop, and was always appropriate to his stage of maturity. It was his perfect God-consciousness that gave Jesus his uniqueness and separated him from all other people. Because of the nature of human sin, which Schleiermacher described as God-forgetfulness, no human being except Jesus has possessed perfect God-consciousness and embodied it in the world.

Schleiermacher's selection of the idiom of "God-consciousness" for his Christology left a lasting impact on nineteenth- and twentieth-century Christology. Throughout the modern period, there have been various attempts to determine Jesus' self-consciousness or understanding of himself, and most of these attempts were inspired, at least indirectly, by Schleiermacher. Many theologians thought that if they could determine the nature of Jesus' self-understanding, they would have a clue to the meaning of the claim that God was "in him."

Schleiermacher was by no means the only theologian to use the idiom of God-consciousness in Christology. It was a common theme in nineteenth-century German theology, and it has even emerged in recent discussions. In the debate in England in the late 1970s concerning the meaning of incarnation and its role in Christian theology, one of the leading participants, John Hick, proposed that what was distinctive about Jesus was the intensity of his consciousness of God. Hick argued that Jesus was so acutely aware of God that he could speak of God with remarkable authority. Like Schleiermacher, Hick has used the idea of God-consciousness for the reinterpretation of the basic claims about Christ.

There are several advantages to the use of the term "God-consciousness" to describe Jesus' relation to God. In the first place, the term clearly protects the humanity of Jesus. Christologies that begin with Jesus' consciousness are not driven to the unfortunate position of dividing Jesus into parts or even natures. They begin with the one reality of human consciousness and argue that Jesus is unique in that his consciousness was determined wholly by his sense of the presence and reality of God. Secondly, the use of the term "consciousness" is more familiar and intelligible to contemporary people than the categories of nature and substance. This term is compatible with the modern understanding of human identity, which involves developmental and psychological categories.

But there are also serious problems in Christologies that appeal to Jesus' God-consciousness, in either their nineteenth-century or their contemporary form. The initial problem, of course, is that New Testament scholarship has demonstrated the difficulty, if not the impossibility, of determining anything about Jesus' consciousness of God or, for that matter, Jesus' consciousness of anything else. As we saw in Chapter 2, the Gospels are not biographies but are proclamations of Easter faith, and as such they do not give access to the historical Jesus' intentions, motives, or self-understanding, or to his consciousness.

From another perspective, it is not clear that the appeal to Jesus' God-consciousness is an improvement on the classical creeds. In the case of Hick, it may be that his view of Christ is finally a modern version of Ebionitism. The early church clearly wanted to say something more than that Jesus' consciousness was shaped by a perfect God-consciousness. The classical creeds affirmed that in his person and his acts Jesus was the reality of God embodied in human form. Jesus was not simply acutely aware of the presence of God, but in his person he was the presence of God's grace and love in the world. Also, Christologies erected on Jesus' God-consciousness have not been any more successful than their classical predecessors in explaining what the early church called "the hypostatic union"—the union of the divine and the human in the one person Jesus of Nazareth. Neither Schleiermacher nor Hick has explained how Jesus' consciousness is shaped by a perfect God-consciousness without lapsing into two forms of consciousness in Jesus.

A second major proposal in contemporary Christology appeals to the experience of redemption or salvation as that is mediated by Jesus of Nazareth or by the Christ of the New Testament. This proposal has appeared in numerous and varied forms during the past two hundred years, but what most of these proposals have in common is an emphasis on the experience of redemption, attributed to Jesus Christ, as the basis of the church's confession that God was in Christ. Schleiermacher laid the foundations for this proposal by describing the New Testament picture of Jesus as the means by which the church interprets its experience of redemption. In most versions of this interpretation of Jesus, the emphasis falls more on the contemporary church's experience of redemption than it does on the historical Jesus.

In the nineteenth century, this proposal was developed in the theology of Albrecht Ritschl (1822–1889), who, like Schleiermacher, described Jesus of Nazareth as uniquely conscious of a new relation to God that was expressed in the symbol of the kingdom of God. Jesus' disciples and subsequent Christian communities experience the meaning and reality of that kingdom in their imitation of Jesus, who is the prototype of humanity's spiritual vocation. And it is the Christian community's experience of redemption that is the basis of its claim that God was in Christ.

Two quite different versions of this form of Christology are those of the Protestant theologian Rudolf Bultmann (1884–1976) in Germany and the Roman Catholic theologian Edward Schillebeeckx in the Netherlands. For Bultmann, the basis of Christian faith and theology is the en-

counter between individuals and the Christian proclamation of God's Word. If people respond in obedience and
faith to the preached Word, then they experience the love
and freedom to live in the world as though they were not
of the world. In the early church, it was the experience of
faith in response to the cross that was the foundation of
Christian preaching. And in the contemporary church it
is the same experience of faith in response to the proclaimed Word that is the basic Christian reality.

In his massive volumes, *Jesus* (1974) and *Christ* (1977),
Schillebeeckx has also focused his attention on Christian
experience, but, unlike Bultmann, he has attempted to
establish a connection between Jesus' own experience—
especially what Schillebeeckx calls Jesus' "Abba experience"—and the experience in the early Christian community of the abiding presence of Jesus, even after his crucifixion, and the expectation of his return.

In each of these proposals, it is Christian experience that
is the basis of the church's claim that Jesus is the incarnation of God's Word. This proposal has a number of
strengths. On the one hand, most versions of this form of
Christology recognize the close relation between confessions about Jesus and an experience of and understanding
of redemption. For the most part, they pay less attention
to philosophical questions about the relation of deity and
humanity in Jesus than they do to the experience of faith
and redemption and the sense in which Jesus of Nazareth
or the Christ of Scripture can be said to mediate that
experience. These theologians readily recognize that discussions about Christology which do not illumine the experience of Christian faith are of little or no interest to
most people in the church. In addition, they recognize
that experiential categories are still meaningful to many
people, while metaphysical and ontological categories are
not.

In many respects, interpretations of Jesus based on the

experience of salvation only reflect a number of important developments that have occurred since the Enlightenment. Perhaps the most important of these is that the primary criterion for determining the truth of an assertion has become internal. Personal experience in the modern age has become perhaps the primary criterion for determining both the meaning and the truth of anything, and Christologies of the type we are discussing only reflect that fact. That is one reason why theologians today give little attention to traditional authorities, such as history and metaphysics, and devote a great deal of attention to personal experience and its immediately related disciplines.

While versions of this interpretation of Jesus recognize the inseparability of Christology and soteriology, they also have encountered serious difficulties. Two are especially important. In shifting the emphasis from the person of Jesus to the Christian experience of redemption, this form of Christology has raised the question of the dispensability of the Jesus of history and perhaps even the Christ of Christian faith. If the primary reality in Christian faith is the experience of redemption, then it is not always clear why Jesus is necessary for the mediation of that experience. If Jesus is simply an example of that experience, then contemporary Christology is making claims fundamentally different from those of the classical creeds. Secondly, even if Jesus is in some way necessary for the mediation of redemption, it often sounds as though it is the experience that identifies who Jesus is rather than Jesus being the means by which one identifies the experience. In classical Christology, statements about Jesus Christ are tied to Christian claims about the experience of salvation, but at the same time it is Jesus Christ who identifies what Christians mean by salvation. In some forms of the charismatic movement, it often does seem as though the experience is the criterion by which one identifies Jesus Christ. That is by no means true of all forms of charismatic Christianity, but where it is true it is a serious threat to Christian faith, because Christians insist that the Spirit is always the Spirit of Jesus Christ, and he is the criterion by which one may "test the spirits" (I John 4:1).

A third contemporary interpretation of Christ is that which has emerged in liberation theology, especially in the black community and in Latin America. In many ways, liberation Christology is similar to the first two types of Christology we have examined. There is no one form of liberation Christology, but most versions of it point to the experience of liberation as the constitutive reality of Christian faith. And in most forms of liberation theology Jesus is understood to be *the* liberator, who defines the meaning of liberation and calls the church to become a community of liberation. Most theologies of liberation insist that what Christians mean by liberation has a historical referent in Israel's experience of the exodus from Egypt and, most important, in the ministry and death of Jesus of Nazareth. An axiom of liberation theology is that one begins with the historical situation in which one finds oneself. And at the same time, an investigation of Christian faith also begins with the historical events that are its foundation. It is not surprising, therefore, that liberation theology is far more interested in the life and ministry of Jesus than it is in speculation about the meaning of the incarnation. It is more interested in discipleship and what it means to follow Jesus than in the reinterpretation of the hypostatic union and the relation of the two natures in the one person Jesus Christ.

Of the many books on liberation theology that have appeared recently, perhaps the most important in the area of Christology has been Jon Sobrino's *Christology at the Crossroads* (1978). Interestingly, Sobrino, a Jesuit priest who teaches in El Salvador, does not devote a single chapter to the theme of liberation. Rather, liberation is the single theme that emerges from several chapters on the historical Jesus. Like most other liberation theologians, Sobrino believes it is very important that Christology begin with what can be known about the historical Jesus, Jesus' proclamation of the kingdom, and what Sobrino calls "the faith of Jesus." It is only by focusing on the historical Jesus that one learns the distinctive features of Christian liberation, and it is the historical Jesus who is the basis of Christian faith and discipleship. Sobrino, like some of the theologians in the first two models we examined, does think it is possible and important to say something about Jesus' developing consciousness. But Sobrino does not turn his back on classical Christology. He argues that there are essential weaknesses in the Chalcedonian formula, but he also acknowledges its abiding significance. In place of Chalcedon's description of "two natures in one person," Sobrino prefers to speak of Jesus' personal oneness with the Father, a oneness Jesus expressed in the radical way in which he lived "for" other people and identified with the poor and the oppressed.

In addition to Sobrino's work, important contributions to liberation theology have been made by feminist theologians (Letty Russell and Rosemary Ruether in the United States) and by theologians from the black church. Perhaps the best-known black theologian is James H. Cone, whose book *God of the Oppressed* (1975) carefully develops the argument that Jesus is black.

> My point is that God came, and continues to come, to those who are poor and helpless, for the purpose of setting them free. And since the people of color are his elected poor in America, any interpretation of God that ignores black oppression cannot be Christian theology. The "blackness of Christ," therefore, is not simply a statement about skin color, but rather, the transcendent affirmation that God has not ever, no not ever, left the oppressed alone in struggle.

Liberation Christology has already performed an important service to the church by reminding it that questions about the true identity of Jesus of Nazareth are also questions about the radical nature of discipleship. Liberation Christology has reminded the church of the difficult gospel Jesus preached. If that gospel were presented in all its offensiveness, there would probably be many people in the church with great possessions who would turn away from Christian faith in sorrow. Liberation Christology will not allow the church, especially the church in affluent cultures, to domesticate the gospel.

But at the same time, it must be said that liberation theology has not yet provided convincing evidence that it is both ethics and theology. Sobrino's book is a step in that direction, but, before a final verdict can be given, liberation theology must tackle some of the difficult classical theological issues, such as the relation of God to the world, and the union of the two natures in the one person Jesus Christ. Theology must not be isolated from ethics, but at the same time ethics cannot serve as a substitute for theological reflection.

A final form of contemporary Christology is that which begins "from below," with the historical Jesus, and discovers his uniqueness and significance as Lord in his openness to God and his complete dedication to the coming kingdom of God. This interpretation of Christ, like the other three we have discussed, does not begin with the incarnation, but with Jesus of Nazareth in his historical particularity. It also pays special attention to the central role the kingdom of God plays in Jesus' ministry, and it does not evade either the early church's claim that the kingdom is near or the need to reinterpret that claim in terms intelligible to twentieth-century people. Language about Jesus' "openness" to God and the future has provided these interpretations of Christ with an idiom for reinterpreting first-century language.

One of the compelling versions of this interpretation of Christ is Wolfhart Pannenberg's *Jesus—God and Man*

(1964). Pannenberg insists that it is the resurrection that unveils Jesus' true identity. Jesus does not become the Christ in the resurrection. That would suggest that Jesus was "adopted" by God as the Christ. But the resurrection does reveal to the world who Jesus truly is and has been throughout his life and ministry. The resurrection, Pannenberg argues, raises the question of Jesus' true identity, a question that the early church answers by means of the incarnation and the nativity stories in Matthew and Luke. The resurrection returns the early church to the teaching of Jesus about the coming kingdom of God and Jesus' openness and obedience to that mission. While the cross called into question Jesus' proclamation of the kingdom, God's raising of Jesus from the dead vindicated Jesus' obedience to that mission. What one sees in Jesus' ministry is a radical openness to the world which has its source in Jesus' openness to God.

Christology must not begin, Pannenberg insists, with the abstract question of how one person can be both human and divine. In other words, it must not begin with the incarnation. Rather, it must begin with the specific man Jesus and the church's understanding of him. It is only in his particular historical context that the church can ask and answer the question of his identity, and it is only in this context that it can make clear its confession that this particular person is both truly human and the presence of the very reality of God.

There are a number of advantages to this approach. On the one hand, it provides compelling insights into the structure of New Testament faith and bases theological reflection on what can be known about the Jesus of history. Its theological categories have a clear referent in the historical events that give Jesus of Nazareth his identity. Also, this form of Christology takes seriously the theme of the nearness of the kingdom in Jesus' gospel, and it provides a way to interpret Christ in modern concepts.

Perhaps it is because this interpretation of Christ takes the New Testament emphasis on the nearness of the kingdom so seriously that one of the major weaknesses in Pannenberg's position is that it does not emphasize the inseparable relation in the Gospels between Christology and discipleship. His Christology says very little about the implications of Jesus' openness to God for Christian discipleship or for the mission of the church in the world. And while one of the strengths of Pannenberg's position is its attempt to reinterpret first-century theology, it is not self-evident that "openness to the future" is an adequate interpretation in the twentieth century of what the early church meant by the nearness of the kingdom.

These four versions of contemporary Christology share a number of features. With the exception of Bultmann's, each appeals to some aspect of the historical Jesus. Rather than beginning with a metaphysical statement about the Logos or the incarnation, they each begin with the historical Jesus—his consciousness, an experience of redemption attributed to him, his liberating activity, his openness to the future—and erect their interpretations of his identity as the Christ on the details of his historical particularity. Furthermore, each of these interpretations recognizes that statements about Jesus' person cannot be separated from a description of his work or ministry. They do not attempt philosophical speculation about Jesus' person without first establishing what Jesus' ministry represents. To be sure, they differ on what is the center of Jesus' gospel —the experience of redemption, the coming kingdom of God, or solidarity with the poor and the oppressed—but each recognizes that Jesus' true identity cannot be separated from what he does. And these interpretations are distinctly modern in that they acknowledge the problems of classical Christology and search for an appropriate way to confess Jesus' identity in contemporary culture.

The last feature of these interpretations—their search

for appropriate language—may also be their major weakness. We have seen that there are serious difficulties in each of the theologies that have been proposed—God-consciousness, the experience of redemption, the struggle for liberation, and openness to the future. The question often asked of each of these proposals is whether their reinterpretations of fifth-century language are in fact an improvement over the classical creeds. Even if one concludes that they are not, contemporary Christology still has no choice but to continue its search for an appropriate means by which to confess its faith in the Lordship of Christ in the modern world.

THE NARRATIVE IDENTITY OF JESUS CHRIST

In addition to the four types of contemporary Christology we have examined, another form of Christology has emerged recently. It focuses on biblical narrative as the appropriate means for determining Jesus' identity. "Biblical narrative," of course, can refer to various types of literature in Scripture. This form of Christology is so new that there is not complete agreement among theologians as to which type of narrative should be the primary focus. Some theologians concentrate primarily on the parables of the New Testament as the most important form of biblical narrative. Other theologians insist that the parables cannot be properly interpreted unless they are read in the context of the larger narratives of the Gospels themselves. From the latter perspective, each of the four Gospels is a story or narrative. Clearly, the Gospels contain different kinds of literature that are not narrative, teachings, commandments, prayers, hymns, etc., but the larger framework of each Gospel is a story with characters, plot, suspense, and the other ingredients that make up a good narrative. To be sure, the Gospel stories are written for different purposes and from quite different theological perspectives, but we profoundly misunderstand them unless we hear and read them as stories about God's grace in Jesus Christ.

Although the Gospels are written from different points of view, at the center of each of them stands the strange figure Jesus of Nazareth. Jesus has a slightly different look about him in each of the Gospels, as we noted in Chapter 2, but in their own way Matthew, Mark, Luke, and John are reciting their stories about Jesus for two common purposes—to tell us why the church confesses him to be the Christ, the anointed one of God, and to remind us what follows from the confession that Jesus is Lord, namely, the nature of discipleship.

Obviously, not everything in Scripture is a story or narrative. Does the focus on biblical narrative mean that some parts of the New Testament—Paul's letters, for example—are irrelevant? Not at all. What Paul gives us are the theological terms and categories for the proper interpretation of the narratives in the Gospels. It may be self-evident to us that the cross of Jesus Christ means that our relationship to God is no longer determined by our perfect observance of the law. In the early church, however, that was not self-evident. Paul tells us that the cross and the narratives in which we encounter it mean that we are justified by God's grace in Jesus Christ and not by our perfect observance of the law. Paul's letters, therefore, are indispensable for a proper interpretation of the meaning of the Gospels.

Narrative Christology is similar in some ways to types of contemporary Christology we have already examined, but it also differs from them in several important respects. It is similar in that most forms of narrative theology do not turn to metaphysical categories (terms such as "being" and "substance") for the interpretation of the union of two natures in the one person Jesus Christ. Although Scripture does not directly answer many of the questions that evoked the church's creeds and confessions, some theologians have noted that Scripture shares a general concern with many of the church's creeds—namely, the question of Jesus' true identity. And, most important, Scripture answers that question very differently than do most creeds and confessions. The New Testament Gospels do not identify Jesus by means of theological propositions and philosophical categories. Rather, they identify Jesus by means of carefully constructed narratives that report and interpret the decisive events in his personal history. While the creeds make theological assertions, the Gospels tell stories, and the two modes of discourse are quite different.

Narrative Christology is not simply a form of storytelling, not simply a matter of repeating Gospel stories about Jesus. But it does work with Scripture differently than do other forms of Christology, both classical and contemporary. Almost every theological interpretation of Jesus claims to be guided and informed by the witness of Scripture. Narrative Christology, however, takes biblical narrative as its primary evidence and attempts to answer questions about Jesus' identity by working directly with Scripture.

An important difference between narrative Christology and other contemporary interpretations of Jesus is that narrative Christology does not attempt to get behind the stories of the Bible to the historical Jesus. It begins with the conviction that the basis for Christology is not some elusive figure who stands *behind* Scripture but the figure identified *in* Scripture. On the one hand, this conviction recognizes Scripture for what it is—a confession of faith and not a biography. At the same time, some forms of narrative Christology do not clarify the historical character of biblical narrative, and thereby create serious theological problems. Both Karl Barth and Hans Frei, for example, argue that biblical narrative is neither history nor nonhistory, but a curious form of narrative which Frei describes as "history-like." The theological problem which such a claim creates is that it appears to call into question the basic Christian assertion that God's redemptive activity has taken place in specific events of human history. If the basis for identifying Jesus and the meaning of salvation is a narrative that is not history but only history-like, it follows that the events of redemption are also not history but only history-like. Such a claim could be interpreted as a form of Docetism and would be vulnerable to many of the criticisms we discussed in Chapter 3. Not all forms of narrative Christology, however, argue that biblical narrative is history-like. It is possible to agree that primary attention should be given to what biblical narrative says about Jesus Christ, but at the same time to acknowledge that the focus is on a historical figure who stands behind the narrative. A narrative Christology of this sort would employ the methods of both literary and historical analysis of Scripture.

How does narrative Christology identify Jesus as the Christ? One answer to that question is provided by Hans Frei's book *The Identity of Jesus Christ.* Frei believes that the Gospels give the reader a story that identifies Jesus, and the narrative unfolds by means of stages. The first stage consists of the birth and infancy stories about Jesus. In this initial stage, Jesus does not really have his own identity. As we noted in Chapter 2, the Nativity stories direct our attention to the history of Israel as the necessary context for understanding Jesus. The history, traditions, and faith of Israel give Jesus his identity. He is not an individual in his own right, but the history of Israel writ small in the person of a single Jewish child. Jesus is the fulfillment of the prophecies of Israel, but it is primarily those prophecies which identify Jesus.

The second stage of the narrative extends from Jesus' baptism by John the Baptist to his decision to carry his ministry to Jerusalem. In this stage of the story, Jesus begins to appear as an individual in his own right. He is the one who appears in Galilee preaching the kingdom of God and engaging in activity that points to its immediate reality. Here Jesus is much more of a distinct individual than he was in the infancy stories, but Jesus is still not yet fully an individual in his own right. Jesus is the one who proclaims and manifests the kingdom of God, but it is the kingdom which gives Jesus his identity.

The third and final stage of the story is Jesus' passion and resurrection. Here the wheel comes full circle. In the events of his trial, his crucifixion, and especially his resurrection, Jesus is most fully himself. Frei points out that it is at this point in the Gospel story that the true meaning of the Christological titles is disclosed. It is no longer the titles of Christ and Messiah that identify Jesus. Now it is Jesus, crucified and risen, who discloses the true meaning of the titles. The Christ is the crucified Jesus. Similarly, it is no longer the theme of the coming kingdom of God that gives Jesus his identity as in the second stage of the story. Now it is the crucified and resurrected Jesus who identifies the kingdom. Jesus Christ is revealed to be the kingdom of God. And finally, it is no longer Israel who gives Jesus his identity as in the first stage of the story. All the promises of God to Israel come to fruition in Jesus, and it is Jesus who is now seen to be the destiny and identity of Israel.

Although Jesus' identity is fully disclosed only in the final stage of the story, the final stage cannot be separated from the first two stages. Jesus is most fully himself in his death and resurrection, but the final stage of the story is unintelligible apart from the rest of the narrative. An important reversal takes place in the passion and resurrection and Jesus becomes who he truly is, but the infancy stories and the history of Israel and the ministry and the preaching of the kingdom are indispensable events in the story. Without them, the reversal would not be possible, and Jesus' identity as the Crucified One would have nothing to do with the history of Israel and Jesus' ministry which embodied the coming kingdom of God. We have already discussed some of the dire consequences of separating the cross and resurrection from Jesus' teaching and healing ministry. If the final stage of the story is separated from the second stage, from the story of Jesus' embodiment of the kingdom, then the church runs the high risk of forgetting that Christology and discipleship are inseparable in the gospel story.

Finally, narrative Christology offers some tantalizing clues for the reinterpretation of the incarnation. What does it mean to say that "in Christ God was reconciling the world to himself"? From the perspective of narrative Christology, that central Christian confession does not mean that there was some part of Jesus of Nazareth that was divine. The incarnation does not refer to the unity of two different parts, one divine and the other human. The incarnation means quite simply that the narrative identity of Jesus Christ, as given in Scripture, is also the disclosure of the identity of God. The Gospels not only identify Jesus, but they identify him as the enacted intentions of God. The identity of any person takes the form of a narrative, and the incarnation is the Christian confession that the biblical narratives about Jesus disclose the identity of God. Jesus is most fully himself in the resurrection because in that single event God's deepest intentions are identified with the person of Jesus of Nazareth. In the Gospels, the resurrection directs the reader's attention back to the story as a whole, and it underlies the Christian confession that in Jesus' narrative identity the world has to do with the identity of God.

Like the other forms of contemporary interpretations of Jesus we have examined, narrative Christology has suggested new possibilities for the reinterpretation of the church's confessions, but it also has created problems which have yet to be resolved. Not the least of these is the elusive character of the term "narrative." Often when theologians use the term "narrative" it is not clear what they have in mind. In the case of narrative Christology, for example, the term "biblical narrative" is sometimes used to refer to specific biblical texts and at other times it appears to refer to a "narrative" that cannot be identified with any specific text in Scripture but somehow is a combination of all biblical narratives and the true meaning of each. The biblical narrative which gives Jesus his identity is not just Mark and not just John but a narrative that cannot be strictly identified with either Gospel but incorporates both. This ambiguity in the use of the term "biblical narrative" is related to the ambiguity of the historical character of the narrative. If biblical narrative is finally something that cannot be identified with any written text, it also has a problematic relation to historical fact.

These are a few of the difficult problems that narrative Christology must still resolve. At the same time, narrative Christology has provided one interesting possibility for the reinterpretation of the church's classical creeds and traditional claims about Jesus, the incarnation, and the meaning of salvation. Protestant theology has often discovered that when it has encountered an apparent impasse, the resolution of that dilemma is found in a fresh return to Scripture and its witness to Jesus as the Christ.

5
PROPHET, PRIEST, AND KING

One of the most attractive features of narrative theology is that it responds to questions about the identity of Jesus Christ by turning first to Scripture. Questions about Jesus' identity cannot be answered simply by repeating biblical stories, but those stories are the church's primary resource for theological reflection about Jesus Christ. Even if Christology begins with biblical narratives, it still must develop categories by which it interprets them, and the categories used by a Christology for the interpretation of Scripture are often its most distinctive characteristic. One question that must be asked of every Christology is whether it illumines biblical narrative. As we noted in Chapter 3, an objection that some people have to the language used in the classical creeds is that it seems unrelated to the content of biblical narratives.

The church has seen various categories proposed for the interpretation of Scripture's narratives about Jesus. One set of categories that may continue to have contemporary significance was first proposed by the Reformers of the sixteenth century. In his *Institutes of the Christian Religion,* John Calvin used the categories of prophet, priest, and king to interpret the identity of Jesus Christ. These categories illumine a number of important themes in classical Reformed Christology. In the first place, the categories are derived from the Old Testament, and they reflect a conviction that Jesus Christ cannot be understood properly apart from God's covenantal history with Israel. The God who raised Jesus from the dead is the same God who led the people of Israel out of Egypt, the God of Abraham, Isaac, and Jacob. To know who Jesus is and what it means to call him the Christ is to know him as the fulfillment of Israel's covenant with Yahweh. The dominant figures in Israel's history are its prophets, priests, and kings, and Christians confess that in Jesus Christ these offices are both consummated and redefined.

When interpreted in the context of the Gospel narratives, the three "offices" of prophet, priest, and king function in a twofold fashion. They provide an interpretation of the meaning of the Gospel narratives about Jesus, and they are in turn redefined by those narratives. The Gospel narratives reveal Jesus to be prophet, priest, and king, but they also demonstrate that he exercises those offices differently than any other prophet, priest, or king in Israel's history. Without the Old Testament, it would be difficult to explain what is meant when Jesus is described by means of these three offices. At the same time, Jesus is not just another of Israel's prophets, priests, and kings. He is unlike any other in Israel's history and provides the definitive meaning for each of these offices.

Each of these offices must be examined in relation to the Gospel narratives about Jesus because these narratives remind us that the full identity of Jesus as the Christ is known only by means of all three offices. Just as Jesus' identity cannot be reduced to a single aspect of the Gospels' narratives (nativity, ministry, or passion), so too it would be a mistake to understand Jesus as only prophet, priest, or king. All three offices are necessary for the proper identification of him, just as the full narrative in the Gospels is necessary in order to understand what is meant by the confession that he is the Christ. He is not simply a prophet, even *the* prophet. Nor is he only a priest, nor only a king. He is all three, and he exercises each of these offices in a unique and particular manner.

FAITHFUL PROPHET

In Chapter 2, we discussed Jesus' relation to the law of Israel and his similarities to and differences from Israel's prophets. Israel's prophets—people like Isaiah, Jeremiah, and Ezekiel—are the bearers of Yahweh's Word to Israel. The prophets preface their statements to Israel with the words "Hear the word of the LORD of hosts" (Isa. 39:5) or "Thus says the LORD" (Isa. 38:1). Christians believe that Jesus also speaks God's Word, but not in the sense that his words are a report or repetition of God's Word. Jesus is not just another of Israel's prophets. While the prophets preface their statements with "Thus says the LORD," Jesus of Nazareth begins his teaching by saying something that none of Israel's prophets would have dared to say. Jesus reminds his listeners of what Israel's law teaches them, and then says, "But I say to you" (Matt. 5:21–48). Jesus claims an authority for himself and his words that none of Israel's prophets would have claimed for themselves. And from its vantage point, after Jesus' death and resurrection, the Christian community makes an even more remarkable claim about him. In its Scripture and in its creeds, the church confesses that Jesus is not only a messenger of God's Word but the very reality of God's Word in human history. Hence John's Gospel affirms:

> And the Word became flesh and dwelt among us, full of grace and truth; we have beheld his glory, glory as of the only Son from the Father. (John 1:14)

The church confesses Jesus to be not simply a man who speaks God's Word to the world but the flesh-and-blood embodiment of that Word.

Two important differences between Jesus and the rest of Israel's prophets are, first, that Jesus claims the authority of God, and, secondly, that his acts are as significant as his words. In the first place, Jesus identifies himself with God's will or intention not only in John's Gospel, where the identification of Jesus and the Word is explicit, but even in the other Gospels. Jesus offers himself and his ministry as a sign of God's kingdom. When the disciples of John the Baptist approach Jesus and ask if he is the Messiah, the long-awaited one, Jesus does not argue with them or offer his teaching as a sign; rather, he says:

> Go and tell John what you hear and see: the blind receive their sight and the lame walk, lepers are cleansed and the deaf hear, and the dead are raised up, and the poor have good news preached to them. And blessed is he who takes no offense at me. (Matt. 11:4–6)

Unlike the prophets, who usually direct attention away from themselves and toward Yahweh, Jesus, through his words and deeds, has an authority unknown in the history of Israel. Jesus does not simply announce God's Word to Israel; in his words and deeds he is God's Word.

When John Calvin discusses Jesus' function as prophet, he interprets it primarily as a teaching office. In this context, Calvin quotes Col. 2:3 ("in him are hid all the treasures of wisdom and knowledge"), and describes Jesus as teaching perfect doctrine which has brought an end to all prophecies. That interpretation of the prophetic office, however, emphasizes Jesus' teaching and fails to recognize the importance of the rest of Jesus' ministry. Jesus differs from the rest of Israel's prophets in that he is God's Word both in what he says and in what he does. As we have seen, he answers John's disciples by pointing to what he does rather than what he says. And it is significant that in Luke's Gospel Jesus begins his ministry in his hometown, Nazareth, by standing in the synagogue and reading from Isaiah:

The Spirit of the Lord is upon me,
because he has anointed me to preach good news to the
    poor.
He has sent me to proclaim release to the captives
and recovering of sight to the blind,
to set at liberty those who are oppressed,
to proclaim the acceptable year of the Lord. (Luke 4:18–19)

And, after reading, Jesus sits down and says, "Today this scripture has been fulfilled in your hearing" (Luke 4:21). It is fulfilled not simply because Jesus reads the text but because in both his words and deeds Jesus is good news, liberation, and the coming of God's kingdom.

An important aspect of Jesus' prophetic office is that his words are inseparable from his actions. In the Gospel narratives the two are interrelated and the one cannot be isolated from the other. That unique feature of Jesus' prophetic office is just as important for our understanding of the church as it is for our Christology. If fundamental questions about the nature and mission of the church are best answered by turning to Jesus Christ, who is Lord of the church, then the inseparability of word and deed in Jesus' ministry has significance for our understanding of the church and questions such as the meaning of evangelism and the church's relation to its social and political order. The church is not an extension of the incarnation, but it does seek to be faithful to the one it calls "Lord." While neither the church nor individuals in it can ever duplicate Jesus' faithfulness, Christians are called to follow Jesus in both their personal and communal existence. That means, in part, that the church must strive to make its teaching and proclamation obvious in what it does in the world. It is not sufficient for the church to restrict its ministry to proclamation. In the New Testament, proclamation is not merely the act of preaching; it also includes witness and ministry. A church that is faithful to Jesus Christ cannot simply preach good news to the poor and release to the captives It must also be involved in the liberation of the poor and the oppressed from their bondage. The church does so not because it identifies with any particular political movement or ideology, but because the Lord it follows calls his disciples to serve him in "the least of these my brethren" (Matt. 25:31–46).

Jesus is, in the words of John's Gospel, "the way, and the truth, and the life" (John 14:6), not because of the wisdom of his teaching and not because of the truthfulness of his acts, but because both his words and his acts are faithful to the God he calls "Abba" and to God's kingdom. In the narratives of the Gospels, Jesus redefines the office of prophet, and in so doing illumines the meaning of faith. In his person and work, Jesus reveals faith to be both unreserved trust and perfect obedience. As the faithful prophet, Jesus wholly trusts in God's grace and faithfulness, exhibits perfect obedience in proclaiming the coming kingdom, and offers a sign of the reality of that kingdom in his own person and ministry.

The temptation stories in Matt. 4:1–11 and Luke 4:1–13 are Scripture's description of Jesus' complete trust in and obedience to God. The temptation stories provide different ways in which Jesus could have been unfaithful. To turn stones into bread would have been to deflect attention from the center of the gospel. The gospel is not the power to perform magic, but the good news of God's coming kingdom and the reign of God's justice and righteousness. For Jesus to have thrown himself down from the Temple would not have been an act of unreserved trust. There is a world of difference between trusting in God's faithfulness and testing the limits that separate God from creation. Jesus recognized the difference between the two, and he refused to play Russian roulette with the tempter. To worship Satan would have been the ultimate act of apostasy, the most flagrant possible acknowledgment that Jesus' trust in and obedience to God was not unreserved. The tempter does not ask Jesus to deny God; he only requests that Jesus also worship him. But Jesus recognizes that the commandment, "You shall worship the Lord your God and him only shall you serve," means that no other reality can receive ultimate trust and obedience.

The Gospel narratives identify Jesus as the faithful prophet who not only reveals the true meaning of faith but also calls his disciples and his church to be faithful, to trust and obey God. As the faithful prophet, Jesus calls the church to attend to both his words and his acts, for together they constitute the one Word of God. Jesus' prophetic office is indispensable for understanding who he is and what his church is called to be and do. He exercises his office in his teaching and ministry, and it is a particular way of being in the world and representing God's kingdom to those in the social order who are without hope that is finally vindicated by God in Jesus' resurrection.

As the prophet of God's kingdom, Jesus is the faithful one. But Scripture will not let us separate our faith in Jesus as the Christ from our response of discipleship. To confess that Jesus is Lord is at the same time to accept the call to take up the cross. A church in which there is much confession of faith but little evidence of discipleship is not a church that takes Jesus Christ or the gospel seriously. As T. S. Eliot reminds us in his "Choruses from 'The Rock'":

> Remember the faith that took men from home
> At the call of a wandering preacher.
> Our age is an age of moderate virtue
> And of moderate vice
> When men will not lay down the Cross
> Because they will never assume it.
> Yet nothing is impossible, nothing,
> To men of faith and conviction.
> Let us therefore make perfect our will.
> O GOD, help us.

The Jesus of the New Testament is anything but a man of moderation. Jesus' invitation—to take up the cross and follow him (Mark 8:34)—is neither practical nor reasonable nor an act of moderation. Any church whose members understand themselves to be disciples of and witnesses to Jesus Christ cannot evade the difficult question of what discipleship means today. "Who is Jesus Christ for us today?" also asks what cross, if any, we have shouldered.

THE PRIEST'S CROSS

The New Testament often refers to Jesus as priest. It understands him to exercise his priesthood in continuity with Israel's priests, but it also knows Jesus to be unlike any priest in the Old Testament. One New Testament text that places major emphasis on Jesus' priestly office is The Letter to the Hebrews, which describes Jesus as "a high priest, holy, blameless, unstained, separated from sinners, exalted above the heavens" (Heb. 7:26).

Like priests in the Old Testament, Jesus "mediates" between God and sinful people. The term "mediator" has often been used in Christian theology to describe Jesus' significance. What is a mediator? In labor arbitration, a good mediator enables two parties in a conflict to understand each other, and the mediator tries to bring about a reconciliation between them. Jesus is the incomparable mediator. In Christian faith and experience, he is the very presence of God's love among us. He re-presents God's grace and love to us. At the same time, Christians confess him to be truly human, like us in every respect except sin. The latter claim is especially important. Were he not "one of us," Jesus could not make God's forgiveness a reality in human life and history. Were he not "without sin," Jesus could not be the occasion for God's grace and forgiveness. As the mediator, he who was without sin takes our sin upon himself and mediates God's forgiveness to us. In

Christian theology, a mediator is not a third creation, part human and part God. The mediator is one person, Jesus of Nazareth, who is truly and fully human, that is, human without the distortion of sin, and who is also truly and fully God, the embodiment of God's grace.

Because of human sin, it is necessary that a mediator present humanity's sacrifices and pleas for forgiveness, and through the mediator God extends forgiveness to a sinful people. As mediator between God and a sinful world, Jesus performs his office in much the same way as did all of Israel's priests:

> For every high priest chosen from among men is appointed to act on behalf of men in relation to God, to offer gifts and sacrifices for sins. (Heb. 5:1)

On behalf of his people, the priest offers gifts and sacrifices to atone for human sin.

Jesus does the same. He is, according to Hebrews, "a high priest for ever after the order of Melchizedek" (Heb. 6:20). But according to the New Testament, Jesus also differs from the priests of the Old Testament in a number of significant ways. Jesus is unlike any of the high priests who have preceded him in that he alone is without sin. While Israel's high priests used blood offerings to atone for the sins of their people and for their own sins, Hebrews claims that Jesus was a high priest "who in every respect has been tempted as we are, yet [is] without sin" (Heb. 4:15). Jesus represents his people before God, yet he is different from them in that he is faithful and without sin. Secondly, Jesus is not a priest by birth. He exercises priesthood as the one chosen by God to be the mediator between God and the world. Thirdly, Jesus offers as an atonement for the sins of the world not the gifts and sacrifices of the people, but himself crucified. And although Hebrews claims that Jesus does continually intercede for us before God, the sacrifice was sufficient and need not be repeated:

> He has no need, like those high priests, to offer sacrifices daily, first for his own sins and then for those of the people; he did this once for all when he offered up himself. (Heb. 7:27)

Like the activity of the Old Testament priests, Jesus' activity as high priest can be summarized by a single word —atonement. Quite literally, he mediates between God and humanity by making them "at one." Jesus is the high priest of Christian faith in that he mediates between God and humanity. He represents humanity before God, and extends to human beings the grace God bestows on him. In his person and the events that give him his identity, Jesus overcomes the sin that separates humanity from God and reconciles the world to God.

Atonement is an important term in the history of Christian theology and has been interpreted in various ways. It has been understood to refer to a cosmic battle fought between God and the devil, in which the latter is tricked and defeated by the crucified Jesus. Atonement has also been interpreted as the payment of a debt by Jesus on behalf of humanity. In this view, God's justice has been offended by human sin, and Jesus expiates the debt and satisfies God's honor and justice by paying the penalty that a sinful humanity could never offer on its own. And the atonement has also been interpreted in less metaphysical categories as a force of moral influence or a moral ideal. Thus interpreted, the cross is not so much a cosmic victory over the devil or the satisfaction of a legal debt as it is an event that should inspire the world and evoke faith.

There are some common themes in these interpretations of the atonement, but also some important differences. Each of them understands sin and humanity's separation from God to be the problem addressed by Jesus' cross and resurrection. Where they differ, of course, is in their interpretations of how sin is "overcome," and even more important, in their understanding of how Jesus' cross alters our relation to God and to each other. The astounding claim made by Scripture is that the death of this first-century Jew does indeed alter our relation to God and to the rest of the world. Most of us would acknowledge that Socrates was a good man who met a tragic and unjust death; yet few, if any, of us would say "Socrates died for my sins." Theories of the atonement are Christian interpretations of how the crucifixion of Jesus of Nazareth places you and me in a new relation to God and to each other.

Must I believe in a particular theory of the atonement in order to be a Christian? What is *the* Christian doctrine of the atonement? The diversity of images used in Scripture to describe the atonement—financial, sacrificial, and legal images—suggests that there is no one appropriate image. Each of these images makes a contribution to our understanding of the redemptive significance of Christ's death. The British writer C. S. Lewis observed that before he became a Christian, he "was under the impression that the first thing Christians had to believe was one particular theory as to what the point of this dying was." After he became a Christian, Lewis learned that his impression was not necessarily true:

> What I came to see later on was that neither this theory nor any other is Christianity. The central Christian belief is that Christ's death has somehow put us right with God and given us a fresh start. Theories as to how it did this are another matter.

That is not to say that the theories are unimportant. Theology is always faith in search of understanding, and for the sake of the gospel it is important that we understand as fully as possible what it is we confess. At the same time, we must not confuse the centrality of Christ's death and the reality of God's forgiveness with the tentativeness of human theories.

What do Christians mean by their claim that Jesus' priestly work is that of at-one-ment, of reconciling us to God? As mediator and agent of atonement, Jesus redefines the Old Testament office of priest. In order to understand how he does this, attention should be directed to the Gospel narratives in which Jesus exercises his priestly office, and above all else to that single event which is the basis of the Christian doctrine of the atonement—the cross.

In the Gospels, the decisive events, but by no means the only significant ones, are the cross and resurrection of Jesus Christ. Both events are indispensable for a proper interpretation of Christian faith, and the one event must not be isolated from the other. Christian faith cannot point to Easter and neglect Good Friday. If it does, it takes human sin less seriously than the Gospels do, and it misrepresents the threat posed by evil. On the other hand, faith cannot concentrate only on Good Friday and ignore Easter. To do so would be to make Christian faith an act of heroic despair and not a gospel of joy and hope. The resurrection in Christian faith is always the resurrection of the Crucified One, and the crucifixion is always the vicious execution of the one God raised from the dead and revealed to be the Christ.

The cross always points to the resurrection, and vice versa, but it is the cross that defines Jesus' activity as priest and explains the meaning of the atonement. An interpretation of Christian faith that ignores Jesus' teaching and ministry, which we have described as Jesus' prophetic office, or that ignores the resurrection, is impoverished, but all good Christian theology is done from the foot of the cross. The cross is that single event in the Gospels which unveils the depth of human sin and the radical nature of God's love. Human sin manifests itself in various forms, but its most devastating form is a self-centered existence cut off from the world and relations to other people. This virulent form of pride and selfishness is the dark night of the soul, and it feeds on fear and shuns the light. Pride and fear go hand in hand, and the one reality they cannot tolerate is their opposite, a love that affirms other people and seeks their fulfillment and happiness. Technically, Jesus may have been executed because he posed a serious threat to the religious and political establishment of his day. The Pharisees and the Sadducees may have turned against him because they considered him a blasphemer. The real opposition that Jesus encountered, however, was pride rooted in fear.

In the narratives of the Gospels what is striking about Jesus is the remarkable freedom he exercises, not only in relation to tradition and Jewish religious law but also in his relation to other people. He enters freely into relations with all kinds of people who are considered something less than human by the rest of society. He approaches them with acceptance and affirmation. There appear to be no limits, no reservations, to Jesus' expression of love. It is this radical form of self-giving which brings forth fear and hatred from those mired in self-centered existence. Jesus was executed in fact by soldiers of the Roman army; in reality he was executed by a sinful world that hates what it fears, that cannot tolerate a love that exposes its pride to be a gross distortion of God's intention.

Jesus is the high priest of Christian faith because his cross is the ultimate act of human love in the face of the world's selfishness, fear, and hatred. It is not just the bare fact of Jesus' death that makes the cross the point of atonement and the mediation between God and humanity. If that were the case, then there could be any number of other high priests, as many martyrs as were willing to endure the pain and suffering of crucifixion. But Christians confess that Jesus of Nazareth is the one high priest, who alone has reconciled God and the world. They make that confession because in both his ministry and his death, Jesus is what no other human being has been or can be—one who loves God wholly and freely and reflects that love in his relations with other people and the world. In the Jesus of the Gospels, there is no hint of inordinate self-centeredness, which is what The Letter to the Hebrews means by its claim that he was like us in every respect yet without sinning.

What is overcome, reconciled, and made one in Jesus' cross is the chasm that separates God from the world and human beings from each other. That chasm is created by a selfish human existence that is unable to turn wholly and freely to the other—be it God or the other person—and thus the consequences of sin infect the created order. Jesus is not just a moral and religious example of self-giving love, what the New Testament calls *agape.* In his person and his work, and above all in his cross, he is the reality of *agape.* As the representative of humanity before God, he overcomes the sin that separates humanity from God.

As the high priest of Christian faith, Jesus Christ discloses the meaning of the atonement by making that peculiar form of love Christians call *agape* a reality in his life and death. Christians are not called to carry Christ's cross or to suffer his death. They are called, however, to allow the power of the cross to manifest itself in their personal and communal life. The good news that Christians proclaim is not just that God has overcome sin by means of Christ's cross, but that Christ's cross has also reconciled God and the world and unleashed the power of *agape* in the world.

THE SOURCE OF HOPE

The final office that Jesus exercises is that of king. As was the case with the offices of prophet and priest, Jesus stands in continuity with Israel's kings, but in the particularity of his own narrative identity he also redefines the meaning of that office.

Like Israel's kings, Jesus also is anointed by God. To be anointed as king was a sign that one had been chosen by God. Although Israel did not consider the king a deity, it did hold its kings in high esteem. When given the chance to slay Saul, David refused to do so, saying, "Do not destroy him; for who can put forth his hand against the LORD's anointed, and be guiltless?" (I Sam. 26:9). The king carries God's blessing and, consequently, must be treated with respect and dignity. According to the New Testament, Jesus also was anointed, like Saul and David. The Gospels report that at his baptism by John a dove descended on Jesus and a Voice from heaven declared, "This is my beloved Son, with whom I am well pleased" (Matt. 3:17). But while he is anointed by God, like the rest of Israel's kings, Jesus also differs from them in the way in which he rules and in the nature of his kingdom. Jesus is not just an instrument of God's righteousness and rule; as God's anointed one, he is the presence and the promise of God's kingdom.

It is not, however, Jesus' baptism that establishes him as king. As we have observed previously, it is that dramatic event which Christians call "resurrection" which is the basis of the Christian confession that "Jesus is Lord." What it means to refer to Jesus as Lord can only be answered by examining the Gospel narratives in their entirety, especially from the perspective of the church's Easter faith and experience. If Jesus' identity concluded with the Gospels' descriptions of his crucifixion, then he might be a figure of heroic, even mythic proportions, but he would not be the one Christians call "Lord." He would be, like Socrates, only yet another good person who came to a bad end. And if the final event in the gospel story were Golgotha, it would be difficult indeed to explain what enabled the disciples to overcome their fear and despair, reassemble in Jerusalem, and begin a ministry that would lead inexorably to suffering and persecution for many of them. It is that strange experience which Christians refer to as "Easter" that is the foundation of their claim that Jesus is Lord, God's anointed one, the Christ, and that forgiveness of sin and the power of sacrificial love are now realities in the world.

Precisely what Christians mean by "resurrection" or for that matter what Scripture means by the term is not always clear, or at least not as clear as some people want. Once again we have an instance where the meaning of an event is more important to Scripture than a precise analysis of its details. The problem, quite simply, is that no one witnessed the resurrection. In the New Testament there are two sets of stories that are the basis of Scripture's claim that God raised Jesus from the dead. One set of stories describe a series of appearances to various friends and disciples of a figure they recognized to be the crucified Jesus. The reality of the appearances of Jesus immediately after his death and burial was so overwhelming that it led those who witnessed them to conclude that God had raised Jesus from the dead and in so doing triumphed over the forces of evil. On the basis of these appearances many people in the early Christian community eagerly looked forward to that day in which God would disclose to the world that Jesus is the Christ and that the kingdom has come in power and glory.

In addition to the appearance stories in the Gospels, there is a second set of stories that describe the experience of some of the women who knew Jesus when they returned to Jesus' tomb after his burial. The accounts vary, but what the women discover is that Jesus is not in the tomb. In Mark's Gospel the women find a young man dressed in a white robe sitting in the tomb. He tells them that Jesus of Nazareth is risen, and the women flee from

the tomb "for trembling and astonishment had come upon
them; and they said nothing to any one, for they were
afraid" (Mark 16:8).

To what, then, does the term "resurrection" refer? Does
it refer only to the appearances of Jesus to his followers
and disciples? The apostle Paul apparently knows nothing
of a story about an empty tomb (see I Cor. 15:3–7). Or does
the term refer primarily to the fact that Jesus' followers
discovered his tomb to be empty? And if the latter, what
became of Jesus' body? How was it "raised"? Scripture
simply does not answer these questions. What it does say
is that Jesus' disciples had various experiences following
his death which led them to make a threefold confession
—that God raised Jesus from the dead, that in so doing
God revealed him to be the Christ, the anointed one, who
establishes God's kingdom of justice and righteousness,
and that God reigns and will reign over evil and all of
creation.

In Scripture the early Christian community is either
unwilling or unable to say precisely what it means by
resurrection. It can only report the experiences that have
led it to the inference and the confession that God raised
Jesus from the dead. What is significant to the early Christians is not how such an event was possible but what that
event meant for the identity of Jesus of Nazareth. In raising him from the dead, God vindicated the Jesus who
proclaimed the coming of the kingdom and the faithfulness of God. God not only vindicates him but also reveals
him to be Lord and Christ, the very reality of the kingdom
itself.

The resurrection establishes Jesus as Lord, but it also
reveals that Jesus exercises the office of kingship in a
unique way. Neither Jesus' kingship nor the kingdom he
begins is like those of this world. Jesus is the kingdom of
God and he reigns over the world, but he does not reign
by means of unlimited power. He reigns by means of the

power of the cross, by means of sacrificial and self-giving
love, which triumphs over evil. He reigns not by means of
brute strength but by means of a love that never lets go
and that persists even in the darkness of death and noth-
ingness. Just as the cross must not be interpreted apart
from the resurrection, so too the resurrection must always
be understood in its relation to the cross. The Jesus whom
God raised from the dead is the Crucified One, and Jesus
reigns as the Crucified One in the kingdom of God.

Although the resurrection is that event by which God
vindicates Jesus and reveals him to be Lord and Christ, the
resurrection is not the final event in the narrative identity
of Jesus of Nazareth. Jesus' identity as the Christ has been
established once and for all by the resurrection, and God's
kingdom has been established as a reality in him. But
Scripture confesses that what is present is also yet to be,
that although Jesus has been vindicated and the kingdom
of God has come and the reign of evil and death have been
broken, the world still awaits the final realization of the
kingdom, when every knee will bow "in heaven and on
earth and under the earth, and every tongue confess that
Jesus Christ is Lord, to the glory of God the Father" (Phil.
2:10–11). Jesus' identity is no longer in doubt, but his story
is not yet finished. Jesus reigns, but he is also yet to reign,
and his narrative remains unfinished until all things are
brought to God through him (I Cor. 15:28).

It is as king, as the crucified Christ, that Jesus gives
Christian hope its distinctive shape and meaning. Christian hope is neither wishful thinking nor speculation about
an unknown future. Because God has vindicated Jesus by
raising him from the dead, Christians look to the future
not in despair but in confident anticipation that the future,
although unknown, belongs to the God who is faithful and
who has consummated the covenant in Jesus Christ. Christians do not know what the future holds, but they do know
that the promises of God have been made good in Jesus

Christ, who was and is and is yet to be, and that they can face an unknown future confident that God is faithful. Because Jesus reigns, Christians do not fear what is yet to be. Christian hope does not mean that Christians know what awaits them. It does not imply a doctrine of personal immortality, and certainly not a denial of the reality of death. But neither do Christians fear the future. With the apostle Paul, they know that

> if we live, we live to the Lord, and if we die, we die to the Lord; so then, whether we live or whether we die, we are the Lord's. (Rom. 14:8)

The offices of prophet, priest, and king illumine the person and work of Jesus of Nazareth and the meaning of life lived in him, but they do so only when they are used to interpret those Gospel narratives which give Jesus his full and true identity. Jesus is the faithful prophet who announces the coming of God's kingdom in his own person and ministry. He is a loving priest who overcomes the chasm of sin by the power of the cross, the power of self-giving love. And he is the king who has been vindicated by God and now reigns, calling everything in the created order to himself.

To know Jesus as the Christ is to know him in the fullness of his narrative identity, to know him as prophet, priest, and king, to know him as that story which reveals the depth of God's love and the unbounded reach of God's grace.

QUESTIONS FOR DISCUSSION

Chapter 1. JESUS CHRIST AND CHRISTIAN FAITH

1. Of the four reasons given why Jesus Christ stands at the center of faith, which seems the most important to you? What other reasons, in addition to the ones listed, do you think are as important or more important?

2. Consider Dietrich Bonhoeffer's question, "Who is Jesus Christ for us today?" In what ways do you think your answer to this question might differ from that given by Christians in other generations?

3. Examine the language used to describe Jesus Christ in the Nicene Creed and that used in the most recent Presbyterian confessions. Which do you find the most helpful? Why?

Chapter 2. THE JESUS OF THE SCRIPTURES

1. Would your understanding of and commitment to Christian faith be altered by the discovery of Jesus' skeleton? Why?

2. What do you think Christians mean when they pray, "Thy kingdom come"?

3. Why do you think Mark insists that it is only at the foot

of the cross that we can understand what it means to say "Jesus of Nazareth is the Son of God"?

Chapter 3. THE CHRIST OF THE CHURCH

1. What were the most important differences between the Antiochenes' view of Jesus Christ and that of the Alexandrians? Which position is closest to your own?

2. How did Docetism and Ebionitism endanger Christian convictions about the meaning of salvation? What examples of those interpretations of Jesus do you think exist in the church today?

3. The recent Presbyterian statement "A Declaration of Faith" says that Jesus' knowledge was limited by his time and place in history. How do you react to that assertion? Why?

Chapter 4. JESUS AND THE THEOLOGIANS

1. Of the four "types" of contemporary Christology discussed in this chapter, which comes closest to your understanding of the Christian confession that "God was in Christ"?

2. Liberation theologians argue that the Jesus of the New Testament identifies with the poor and the oppressed of the world. Do you think they are correct in their interpretation of Scripture? If they are, what implications does that interpretation of Jesus have for the church's ministry today?

3. In this chapter, an argument is made that the Pauline letters provide us with the theological principles necessary for a proper interpretation of the relation between Paul and the Gospels. What are some examples of Pauline theological principles that are important for our reading and interpretation of the Gospels?

Chapter 5. PROPHET, PRIEST, AND KING

1. The Gospel of Mark reports (Mark 15:34) that Jesus died saying, "My God, my God, why hast thou forsaken me?" Was that a cry of despair or a cry of faith? If it was a cry of despair, how can we continue to speak of Jesus as the faithful prophet?

2. How would you explain to a non-Christian what we mean when we say, "Jesus died for our sins"?

3. Read I Corinthians 15. What does Paul allow us to say about the meaning of Jesus' resurrection for us? In what do Christians hope—the immortality of the soul, the Second Coming of Christ, or the faithfulness of God?

REFERENCES

In this volume reference is made to the following books and periodicals, which are listed in the order of their use:

The Book of Confessions, Part I of *The Constitution of The United Presbyterian Church in the United States of America* (Office of the General Assembly of The United Presbyterian Church in the United States of America, 1970), 1.2 (Nicene Creed) and 9.08 (The Confession of 1967).

Dietrich Bonhoeffer, *Letters and Papers from Prison,* ed. by Eberhard Bethge, Enlarged edition (Macmillan Publishing Co., 1972), p. 279 (30 April 1944).

John A. T. Robinson, *The Human Face of God* (Westminster Press, 1973), and Hans Küng, *On Being a Christian* (Doubleday & Co., 1976).

Philip Melanchthon, "Loci Communes Theologici," in *Melanchthon and Bucer,* ed. by Wilhelm Pauck, Vol. XIX in The Library of Christian Classics (Westminster Press, 1969), pp. 21–22.

Flannery O'Connor, "A Good Man Is Hard to Find," in *The Complete Stories* (Farrar, Straus & Giroux, 1971), p. 132.

John Calvin, *Institutes of the Christian Religion,* ed. by John T. McNeill, Vols. XX and XXI in The Library of

Christian Classics (Westminster Press, 1960), Vol. I, p. 690 (III. vii. 1).

Saint Augustine, *Confessions,* tr. by R. S. Pine-Coffin (Penguin Books, 1961), p. 207.

"The Theological Declaration of Barmen," in *Our Confessional Heritage: Confessions of the Reformed Tradition with a Contemporary Declaration of Faith* (General Assembly of the Presbyterian Church in the United States, 1978), pp. 154–155.

Eduard Schweizer, *Jesus,* tr. by David E. Green (John Knox Press, 1971), p. 16.

J. N. D. Kelly, *Early Christian Doctrines,* 5th rev. ed. (Harper & Row, 1978).

"The Chalcedonian Decree," in *Christology of the Later Fathers,* ed. by Edward Rochie Hardy, Vol. III in The Library of Christian Classics (Westminster Press, 1954), p. 373.

G. K. Chesterton, *Orthodoxy* (1908; Doubleday & Co., Image Books, 1959), p. 92.

Søren Kierkegaard's Journals and Papers, Vol. 1 (A–E), ed. and tr. by Howard V. Hong and Edna H. Hong (Indiana University Press, 1967), p. 125.

Walter M. Abbott (ed.), *The Documents of Vatican II* (America Press, 1966), pp. 220–221.

"A Declaration of Faith" in *Our Confessional Heritage,* pp. 163, 162.

Friedrich Schleiermacher, *The Christian Faith,* ed. by H. R. Mackintosh and J. S. Stewart (Fortress Press, 1977); see especially pp. 374–475.

John Hick (ed.), *The Myth of God Incarnate* (Westminster Press, 1977); see especially Hick, "Jesus and the World Religions," pp. 167–185.

Edward Schillebeeckx, *Jesus: An Experiment in Christology,* tr by. Hubert Hoskins (1974; Seabury Press, 1979); and *Christ: The Experience of Jesus as Lord,* tr. by John Bowden (1977; Seabury Press, 1979).

Jon Sobrino, *Christology at the Crossroads: A Latin American Approach,* tr. by John Drury (Orbis Books, 1978).

James H. Cone, *God of the Oppressed* (Seabury Press, 1975), p. 137.

Wolfhart Pannenberg, *Jesus—God and Man* (1964, E.T. 1968), 2d ed., tr. by Lewis L. Wilkins and Duane A. Priebe (Westminster Press, 1977).

Hans W. Frei, *The Identity of Jesus Christ* (Fortress Press, 1975).

Calvin, *Institutes,* Vol. I, pp. 494–503 (II. xv. 1–6).

T. S. Eliot, *The Complete Poems and Plays, 1909–1950* (Harcourt, Brace & Co., 1952), p. 110.

C. S. Lewis, *Mere Christianity* (Macmillan Co., 1960), p. 42.

FOR FURTHER READING

Baillie, D. M. *God Was in Christ.* 2d ed. Charles Scribner's Sons, 1955.

Barth, Karl. *Church Dogmatics.* Tr. by G. W. Bromiley et al. Edinburgh: T. & T. Clark, 1956–1962. Vols. IV/1, 2, and 3.

Bonhoeffer, Dietrich. *Christology.* Tr. by John Bowden. London: William Collins Sons & Co., 1966. Also published under the title *Christ the Center,* Harper & Row, 1966.

Bornkamm, Günther. *Jesus of Nazareth.* Tr. by Irene and Fraser McLuskey with James M. Robinson. Harper & Brothers, 1961.

Dodd, C. H. *The Parables of the Kingdom.* Rev. ed. Charles Scribner's Sons, 1961.

Hendry, George S. *The Gospel of the Incarnation.* Westminster Press, 1958.

Hengel, Martin. *The Son of God.* Tr. by John Bowden. Fortress Press, 1976.

Jeremias, Joachim. *The Parables of Jesus.* Tr. by S. H. Hooke. Rev. ed. Charles Scribner's Sons, 1971.

Johnson, Robert Clyde. *The Meaning of Christ.* Westminster Press, 1958.

Kasper, Walter. *Jesus the Christ.* Tr. by V. Green. Paulist/Newman Press, 1977.

Kelber, Werner H. *Mark's Story of Jesus.* Fortress Press, 1979.

Moltmann, Jürgen. *The Crucified God.* Tr. by R. A. Wilson and John Bowden. Harper & Row, 1974.

O'Collins, Gerald. *What Are They Saying About Jesus?* Paulist Press, 1977.

Ritschl, Dietrich. *Concerning Christ.* Richmond, Texas: Well-Spring Center, 1980.

Schoonenberg, Piet. *The Christ.* Tr. by Della Couling. Herder & Herder, 1971.

Ziolkowski, Theodore. *Fictional Transfigurations of Jesus.* Princeton University Press, 1972.